BLUE MYTHOLOGIES

BLUE MYTHOLOGIES
Reflections on a Colour

CAROL MAVOR

REAKTION BOOKS

Published by Reaktion Books Ltd
33 Great Sutton Street
London EC1V 0DX

www.reaktionbooks.co.uk

First published 2013
Copyright © Carol Mavor 2013

Printed and bound in China

British Library Cataloguing in Publication Data
Mavor, Carol, 1957–
   Blue mythologies : reflections on a colour.
   1. Blue.
   2. Symbolism of colors.
   I. Title
   155.9'1145-dc23
   ISBN: 978 1 78023 083 2

Contents

For Hayden White

Blue, here is a shell for you
Inside you'll hear a sigh
A foggy lullaby
There is your song from me.

Joni Mitchell, 'Blue'

Carol Mavor, *Untitled* (Canal Water off the Fortuny Museum, Venice),
2010, photograph.

INTRODUCTION:
Paradoxically Blue

paradox

1. *b. Rhetoric. A figure of speech consisting of a conclusion [. . .] contrary to what the audience has been led to expect.*

2. *a. An apparently absurd or self-contradictory statement or proposition, or a strongly counter-intuitive one, which investigation, analysis, or explanation may nevertheless prove to be well-founded or true.*

Oxford English Dictionary

PARADOXICALLY BLUE

Blue Mythologies: Reflections on a Colour is a visual, literary and cultural study of the colour blue. *Blue Mythologies* uncloaks blue as a particularly paradoxical colour. The conflicting temperaments of the blues unravel easily. For instance, blue is the purity of the Virgin Mary, *yet* blue names a movie as obscene. Or, blue is the colour of eternity, *yet* blue lips are a sign of approaching death. The yarn of this book takes up many hues of the colour, *yet* its pattern remains faithful to one 'over and done with' thread: blue is paradoxical; it is self-contradictory, yet true.

MYTHOLOGY ITSELF IS A PARADOX

'Mythology', because it can mean allegory, legend, wisdom, fabulous narration and beliefs that are traditional, collective, particular and cultural, is itself a paradox. 'Mythology' cloaks truth in fiction and fiction in truth. This book sheds light on mythology as hued para-doxically blue. My writing makes good blue's duplicity, as *the* hue of mythology. In the spirit of Roland Barthes' *Mythologies*, my *Blue Mythologies* is the work of an essayist, with an eye on the *novelesque*.[1]

Here is a blue *science fiction mythology*. It is a myth that our blood is blue until it is oxygenated. Rather than the physical proper-ties of the light itself, the blue in our veins is an affect, a cognitive characteristic of the eye and brain. Venous blood is not in fact blue (it is deep red) – however, the light, which is scattered from tissue beneath the vein in the back of your hand, passes through the blood on its way to our eye and emerges from the skin in a way that makes it *appear* blue. The effect has been coined as *Retinex*, a portmanteau word derived from 'retina' and 'cortex'. Retinex theory explains that, when looking at blue veins, the eye and the brain are involved in the processing of seeing. Edwin Land, the developer of 'Polaroid', formulated the concept in 1971. Polaroid blues are amongst the most gorgeous blues I know, like those obscene Polaroid blues of fashion / art photographers Helmet Newton and Guy Bourdin. Land explains why my blood looks blue and gave us the gift of the Polaroid with its stunning instant cyans. This *is* the kind of fluke that a connoisseur of blue can smile over. Colette has written 'there are connoisseurs of blue just as there are amateurs of . . . wine vintages'.[2] I am trying to be a connoisseur of blue.

Here is another blue *science fiction mythology*. It is not a myth that all newborn irises *look blue*, whatever final pigmented colour they may end up with. At birth, the infant's unpigmented iris contains many molecular scatterers in a transparent medium: that is why we see a bluish eye when we look into them. Newborn babies' eyes seem blue; not because they are pigmented, but because they scatter blue light to us. Once the pigment arrives, the iris has effectively been painted, and its colour is then determined by the pigment's absorption properties; not unlike the blue crystals in the starred ceiling of Giotto's Arena Chapel, which absorb colour in white light, leaving only blue to be reflected to us. The blue sky in Wyoming absorbs nothing, but scatters the blue of sunlight down to us; not unlike the newborn eyes of babies. In sum: a baby's blue eyes are scattered light; Paul Newman's true-blue eyes are absorbed light.

My stories seek blue (duplicitous) truths, which nevertheless ring true. In the words of my former teacher Jim Clifford, 'If we are condemned to tell stories we cannot control, may we not, at least, tell stories that we believe to be true'.[3] True as Coventry blue: a 'reference to the blue cloth and blue thread made at Coventry, noted for its permanent dye'.[4]

Unlike Coventry cloth, or Giotto's Arena Chapel frescoes, which do, of course fade, if to a lesser degree than other textiles and frescoes, the blues that derive from the passage of the light itself are independent of dye, paint and time; they are *not* the complement of absorption. The blue of the sky is preferentially scattered towards our eyes from rays of light passing over our heads and interacting with molecules of atmospheric air; these atoms have not changed since the time when Giotto was painting in Padua, when the blue of the sky was exactly as it is now.[5]

I have been to Padua. Coventry is but a two-hour train ride from where I live. Nevertheless, this book has a penchant towards French excursions, particularly when it comes to theory, novels and films. You might say that I have fondness for *French Blue*: a place colour, like Egyptian blue and Prussian blue.

Some of you may be thinking of Barthes' critique of the famous French tourist guides that appeared in his 1957 collection of essays, entitled *Mythologies*. With Barthes' critique of France's *Le Guide bleu* at hand, *Blue Mythologies* is admittedly blue tourism. But like Barthes, I am a travel-writer who resists the 'bourgeois norm'.[6] For Barthes, *and* for *Blue Mythologies*, 'paradox is *not contradiction*; it is a rhetorical strategy, an artistic treatment of a logical problem' (Hayden White).[7]

I AM A MALE SATIN BOWERBIRD

As a connoisseur of blue, like the collectomaniac box artist Joseph Cornell (a magpie for blue), I perform my text like the artistically determined male Satin Bowerbird. Australia's male Satin Bowerbird is famous for constructing and decorating richly decorated bowers, some even with interiors painted blue. Birds of this species have been observed painting with blueberry juice, using crude brushes made of sticks and moss. The blue objects are collected to bring the female bird in. The older and more experienced the male, the better and more beautiful the blue bower. These bowers are bachelor pads for mating; they are not nests for a family. Once copulation has taken place, the female is on her way to a life of single parenthood.

Not that long ago, an ornithologist observed this in just one bower:

Dante Gabriel Rossetti, *The Blue Bower*, 1865, oil on canvas.

Seventy-five blue plastic items including tops from ballpoint pens, plastic pegs, bottle tops, a toothbrush and parts of broken toys, together with fifteen blue-edged feathers . . . ten dried snail shells, several pieces of fawn-coloured twine and two blue marbles. Four longs strands of blue wool were so placed as to lead into and through the 'avenue' [the centre of the bower, which is open on both ends]. Also decorating the platform [the inside floor of the bower] were . . . blue and cream-green flowers . . . and other perishable items, which were replaced during the breeding season. Small blue ornaments, including . . . flowers, were scattered along the floor of the avenue.[8]

In 1865 Dante Gabriel Rossetti painted his beloved Fanny Cornforth in a blue bower. Rossetti's nickname for this blousy redhead bird was 'little elephant'. A plump beauty, with bee-sting lips, if she had lived during our time, she would have sent Lucian Freud into some competitive bower-building. The painting's background of blue-and-white tiles are Orientalized tastes of 'Arab' and 'Chinese'[9] designs. Passion flowers and clinging 'wild convolvulus blossoms'[10] entwine her figure in this Arabian Nights blue bower so as to enhance the passion we feel for her and her emerald green, blue–turquoise trimmed robe, the latter spilling out clouds of soft creamy fur. In the foreground are blue cornflowers, a play on Cornforth's name. She pulls at the strings of a Japanese koto; I hear bluebells, but no wedding bells. A mistress and a housekeeper of Rossetti's, she never did marry the artist. Never for her: 'Something Olde, Something New, Something Borrowed, Something Blue . . .'.

My essays (long and short) are blue bowers that perform the mythology of blue as paradoxical. Like the cornflowers at the entrance of Rossetti's blue bower, ornaments to lead in, let me draw you inside.

1
EVERYTHING IS BLUE

'THE INK THAT I use is the blue blood of the swan' (Cocteau)[1]
that blossoms and blooms into blues within blues, including
Yves Klein's blue *Anthropométries*, Gainsborough's *The Blue Boy*,
the copyeditor's 'blue pencil', the 'blue nose' of morality, 'blue
movies', 'blue stockings', examination booklets and cheese.
My ink bleeds the ice blue of glaciers, the struggle of 'blue collar'
workers, the authority of 'blue coats', the snobbery of aristocratic
'blue blood', the incomprehensible violence of the blue eyes of
the Aryan race of the Nazi regime, the struggles of the 'blueman'
(*blomon*) of the thirteenth and fourteenth centuries who today
would be called a 'black man', the beauty of the scattered light
of the sky and the sea ('the light that got lost'[2]), the crystalline
intensity of the filtered blue of the Virgin's lapis lazuli cloak
in Piero della Francesca's *Madonna del Parto*, the optimism
of the bloom of the aster, the iris in the hands of Vincent van
Gogh, the pursuit of Novalis's blue (mourning) flower and
'the air a fist has bruised'.[3] Sometimes, it seems, that everything
is blue.

In 1972 the *Apollo 17* astronauts took a photograph of
the earth with the sun behind them. Floating in black space,
the earth appeared as a 'blue marble', and they named it as such.
It was the first time on any *Apollo* flight that the astronauts
were made privy to a view of the full earth. Hence, '[s]een from
a great distance, the earth displays different colors, but blue is
largely dominant because of the oxygenation of the surrounding
atmosphere'.[4] Looking at the image, the sea becomes 'that other
sky below the world'.[5] Paul Éluard's surreal, prophetic words,
'the earth is blue like an orange' echo with the haunting words
of the French novelist Marie Darrieussecq, remarking that
'astronauts are trained not to go insane when they see the

Piero della Francesca, *Madonna del Parto* (post-restoration), *c.* 1450–70,
detached fresco.

Earth, round and blue, smaller than their porthole'.[6] More soothing are the words of Rebecca Solnit who poetically claims that 'the world is blue at its edges and in its depths'.[7]

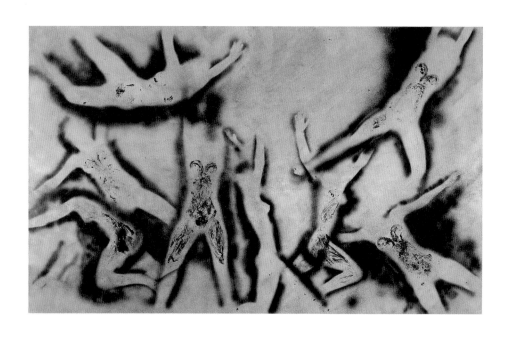

Yves Klein, *People Begin to Fly*, 1961, oil on paper mounted on canvas.

2
BLUE IS JOYFUL-SAD

After walking across the garden of the Arena in the glare of the sun, I entered the Giotto chapel, the entire ceiling of which and the background of the frescoes are so blue that it seems as though the radiant daylight has crossed the threshold with the human visitor in order to give pure sky a momentary breather in the coolness and shade, a sky merely of a slightly deeper blue now that it is rid of the glitter of the sunlight, as in those brief moments of respite when, though no cloud is to be seen, the sun has turned its gaze elsewhere and the azure, softer still, grows deeper. This sky transplanted on to the blue-washed stone was peopled with flying angels . . .

Marcel Proust, *In Search of Lost Time*

WHEN ENTERING THE 'semidarkness' of Giotto's Arena Chapel, 'blue is the first color to strike the visitor'.[1] This was 'unusual in Giotto's time because of its brilliance'.[2] It takes your breath away. One is struck by a feeling of pleasure that is as enchanting as the azure background of the surrounding walls, which gives way to narrative depictions of the lives of the Virgin and Christ. The blue walls are as dazzling as the sapphire ceiling above, which is patterned with stunning stars and roundels of the son of God, his mother and Prophets.

Indeed, in this blue cocoon writ large, Giotto has 'transplanted'[3] the sky on to the walls and ceiling. The paradise above is an unreal, moonlit blue, twinkling with painted gold stars that have been arranged with the skill of a first-class *pâtissier*. The stars appear like Moravian cookies on a vast midnight-blue baking sheet; their divineness is a taste of heaven. To enter the chapel is to fall into another world, a blue one, as blue as our own 'blue marble'. The effect of Giotto's blue is bliss: what Julia Kristeva calls '*jouissance*'. 'Giotto's Joy' is a most-fitting title to Kristeva's essay on the artist's frescoes (1300–1305), perfectly denoting the Florentine painter's radical and breathtaking use of blue.

Curiously, there is 'no rivalry between background and figure':[4] the effect is positively dynamic. The characters (not too large, not too small) tear themselves away from the blue to touch us: they come to us *out of the blue*, while (at the same time) these same figures recede into the blue. Likewise, the blue foundation cascades out to soak us in its pigment. Yet, this nearly unadulterated blue also recedes behind the figures. Figure and ground push and pull (like Hans Hofmann's use of pure colours in his abstract paintings), rise and fall, like a song, like the sea and the sky, like the gloomy contentment of a melancholic, the nostalgic who is joyful-sad.

Giotto's blue gives us wings: we invisibly sprout them, so to speak, and achieve a 'genuine power of flight'.[5] Gliding like an angel, or, even like a student of the great aeronaut Roland Garros, we join celestial creatures in 'looping the loop',[6] as in the panel

Giotto, Angel in the *Crucifixion* (detail), Arena Chapel, Padua, *c.* 1300–05, fresco.

Giotto, *The Baptism of Christ* (detail), Arena Chapel, Padua.

The Pietà. It is as if Yves Klein has gone back in time to miraculously join hands with Giotto. Flying is blue. It is as if Giotto has gone forward in time to miraculously join hands with Yves Klein. Dreamily, I alight into Klein's *Anthropometry* entitled *People Begin to Fly* (1961), made by, perhaps, the bluest artist of all time, a boyish man who really believed that he could fly. ('He was sure he could fly', so claimed his wife.[7])

Giotto's blue gives us a bath, a pool, a sea, a river, as in the panel, *The Baptism of Christ*. Here, the nearly naked, full-length body of Christ stands in turquoise-blue water; its colour is oddly reminiscent of David Hockney's early paintings of Los Angeles pools. These turquoises, swimming-pool blues of Giotto's River Jordan, also evoke those particular cyans of the instant Polaroid picture.

When the magic is instigated back by the instant photo hands of Helmut Newton, the cyans of the Polaroid are titillating. Newton took Polaroids as studies during his fashion shoots, to see what he would get before committing to a shot, but ended up liking the instant images for their own rawness. Amidst the Polaroids, one finds Newton's proclivity for blue satin sheets, the blue of artificial light in the night, blue stilettos, blue lingerie and other illicit blues seeping through barriers. Even the white skin of his exceedingly tall models (with legs like pale gazelles and breasts with pert nipples like pale watchful eyes) take on the hue of blue. Newton celebrated the blue light of his Polaroids by publishing a collection of them in *Pola Woman*: a book of instant sexiness (even if the model was prepared for hours in the staged setting).[8] Newton's blue Polaroids pose in the light of 'blue movies'.

Because it is *privately* self-developed (from a pre-digital age where such ease and spontaneity were novel), the Polaroid is amateur and can be attached to the pornographic. No embarrassment. No threat of an overzealous Fotomat employee contacting the police. One only needs to wait for the picture to slowly and magically emerge before one's eyes.

The Polaroid of a beautiful nude woman by Esther Teichmann (*Untitled*, 2012) is soaked in those same promiscuous blues that we associate with the instant medium, even when depicting whites and blacks. There is an overall blue tint to the woman's otherworldly ivory skin, which is chilled not only by the coolness of the colour but also by thoughts of the morgue. The white stuffed and knotted comforter that she lies on has also taken on the refrigerating blue of this instant process. Her black hair has become indigo, especially those strands that run across her left hand (caught with 'just the right degree of openness, the right density of abandonment'[9]). Her eyes appear to shine out (like a nocturnal animal at night) with a blue that is surprising, given the blackness of her hair. Blue velvet lies underneath this wolf-girl's buttocks and legs. She is in a pool of blues which her body absorbs from head to toe with a bruising, underwater look.[10] Teichmann's picture reflects on the fashion Polaroids of Newton through the eyes of a drowned Ophelia. A fallen angel. She is a Polaroid from heaven. (It was Teichmann who first told me about Polaroid blues.)

Paradoxically, and antithetically to its illicitness, the Polaroid has been instrumental in proving the sightings of contemporary apparitions of the Virgin Mary. These divine pictures, sometimes of a beautiful blue sky, cast in Polaroid blue, with streaks of Marian light are read 'like a religious Rorschach test'.[11] Believers refer to their proofs of Mary's existence as 'miracle photos' or 'Polaroids from Heaven'.[12] A particularly famous site for Marian apparitions is in Flushing Meadows Park in New York City, in the borough of Queens. Folklorist Daniel Wojcik visited the site and has noted not only the visual productions but also the audible experience produced by the fervent pilgrims with 'the sound of the clicking and fluttering camera shutters and then the whirl-buzz of film being ejected from hundreds of Polaroid cameras'.[13] The Polaroid (unlike conventional prints made from a negative or from digital images) cannot be manipulated: it speaks the truth. This 'mistrust in

Esther Teichmann, *Untitled,* 2012, Polaroid. Permission courtesy of the artist.

camera lenses' as 'a distorted translation of reality' stretches back
to the nineteenth century.[14] Yet photographs are used as evidence
of the truth. The answer to the photographic paradox is, at least
for the apparition seekers, the Polaroid, which they view as a gift
from Mary. As Wojcik learned from the miraculous Polo Marians,
'Our Lady gives . . . the miracles in the photos. These are her gifts
from us'.[15] Apparently, Scotch-taping rose petals to the side of
one's camera enhances 'the possibility of taking a miracle photo'.[16]
If only blue roses could be found. But blue roses are impossible.

Jean Baudrillard says this about the magical quality of the
Polaroid:

> The ecstasy of the Polaroid is . . . to hold the object and its
> image almost simultaneously as if the conception of light of
> ancient physics or metaphysics, in which each object was
> thought to secrete doubles or negatives of itself almost simulta-
> neously that we pick up with our eyes, has become a reality.
> It is a dream. It is the optical materialization of a magical process.
> The Polaroid photo is a sort of ecstatic membrane that has come
> away from the real object.[17]

Returning to Giotto's *The Baptism of Christ,* I see a similar
primitive *Polaroidicity* in the spirit of Giotto's fresco.

Above Christ is a flash of light suggesting the magical creation
of an image; like those legends from the nineteenth century
'concerning flashes of lightning imprinting extraordinary images
on glass window panes'.[18] Within the boom of light is the fore-
shortened hand of God, in a delicate pink sleeve. God is reaching
down *out of the blue.* God is in touch (or nearly so) with his secreted
double (Christ, who is man in God's own image). God as, and
within, a flash of light evokes the etymology of photography
(light-writing) and its spirit (saving the dead), centuries before the
medium's invention. With a modern vision towards the photograph,
which he would never know, 'Giotto hearkens . . . the Byzantine-

inspired conception of baptism as *photismos*, literally illumination, and thereby lays stress on the light, both as substance and image'.[19]

In Giotto's blue womb, Christ can be understood in the specific light of the Polaroid photo as 'a sort of ecstatic membrane that has come away'[20] (Baudrillard) from the hand of God. Indeed, the turquoise-cyan water suggests amniotic fluid within the membrane of the amniotic sac in the hue of the Polaroid's particular key. Like a Newton Polaroid, like Teichmann's nude, Christ's skin (at least from the waist down) is bathed in the hue of a cool blue. *The Baptism of Christ* is a fresco that surprisingly conveys the 'ecstasy of the Polaroid'.

Giotto's Arena Chapel is a revolutionary translation of the Gospel and offers *novel* ways to *read* the Bible through juxtaposition. Just as we should not read the panels as separate from the overwhelming blue ground in which they are housed, we should not just read the frescoes as separate pictures. The arrangement of Giotto's Paduan cycle delivers conventional and unconventional links, what Michel Alpatoff calls 'correspondences', in an echo of a Baudelaire not named.[21] As Alpatoff explains:

> The correspondence between the *Crucifixion* and the *Baptism* is obvious. Mediaeval iconography regarded Jordan's water in the Baptism as the prototype of the blood shed by Christ in Golgotha: but the Crucifixion was never juxtaposed with the Baptism.[22]

Giotto makes a correspondence between the red blood of Christ and the blue of the River Jordan. The paradox works through the blue. History quakes: the blue Arena Chapel in Padua lands next to the red House of Mysteries in Pompeii. The point is not to synthesize (to make purple), but rather to keep the correspondence alive, moving, reading, singing, tearing.

Giotto's *Last Judgment* covers the full wall at the Chapel's entrance (taking on the curvature of the barrel vault roof): the top

Angel tearing away the blue in Giotto's *Last Judgment* (detail), Arena Chapel, Padua.

of the arch is flanked with an angel on each side who is tearing away the blue, like a scroll, so as to reveal that this surface is lined with red. 'Abruptly', writes Kristeva, 'the scroll tears . . . exposing the narrative as nothing but a thin layer of color'.[23] Perhaps, but what could be richer than a 'narrative' of blue that is juxtaposed by red?

B. B. King sings the blues with his guitar named Lucille (a name derived from light). He closes his eyes as he plays. The feeling is bluesy, joyful-sad.

In Emily Dickinson's poem, the sound of a buzzing fly sounds blue as the eyes fail:

With Blue – uncertain stumbling Buzz –
Between the light – and me –
And then the Windows failed – and then
I could not see to see –[24]

In Derek Jarman's 1993 film, *Blue* (a goodbye to the world as he dies from AIDS), the voice-over mournfully speaks of the joys of blue. Blinded by the disease, Jarman 'could not see to see'. Blue was the colour Jarman saw when eye drops were put in his eyes, in the hope of alleviating his blindness. Paradoxically, blindness allowed Jarman to see beyond the distraction of images, directly into the realm of colour – as Yves Klein had wished.[25] As viewers of *Blue*, there is nothing to see save for a projection of monochromatic International Klein Blue for the full seventy-five minutes of the film. The soundtrack is Jarman's poetic voice-over and a music score by his collaborator Simon Turner. Gazing into the blue, one hears 'the blues' like this:

Blue bottle buzzing/ Lazy days/ The sky blue butterfly/ Sways on a cornflower/ Lost in the warmth/ Of the blue heart haze/ Singing the blues/ Quiet and slowly/ Blue of my heart/ Blue of my dreams/ Slow blue love/ Of delphinium days'.

HEARING THE BLUE SKY

The contemporary poet Vona Groarke hears the blue sky on the car radio:

JULY

Blue sky on the radio,
all four car windows down.
Is this what it means, then,
to have friends?[26]

Proust can hear the blue of a sunny day, before he even opens his eyes in the morning. As the Narrator, let's call him 'Marcel',[27] of *In Search of Lost Time*, explains:

At daybreak, my face still turned to the wall, and before I had seen above the big window-curtains what shade of colour the first streaks of light assumed, I could tell what the weather was like. The first sounds from the street had told me . . . as soon as I heard the rumble of the first tramcar, I could tell whether it was sodden with rain or setting forth into the blue.[28]

In Francisco de Zurbarán's *The Virgin of Mercy of Las Cuevas* (c. 1644–55), the blue heaven comes down to earth as Mary's blue veil. This Spanish Virgin bowers a field of monks, like praying white rabbits, in an azure of piety. Her mantle is pinned with a huge blue jewel. Along with the monks, we can *hear* the blue.

But Mary did not always wear blue. Before the twelfth century, she might have worn 'black, gray, brown, violet . . . or dark green'.[29] But by the twelfth century, 'blue alone evoked the Virgin's mourn - ing' – while at the same time, 'her blue' became 'brighter and clearer' as 'a form of divine illumination'.[30] For Mary, blue is purely duplicitous: it is the sadness of mourning, tinged with the joyful hope of heaven.

Francisco de Zurbarán, *The Virgin of Mercy of Las Cuevas*, c. 1644–55, oil on canvas.

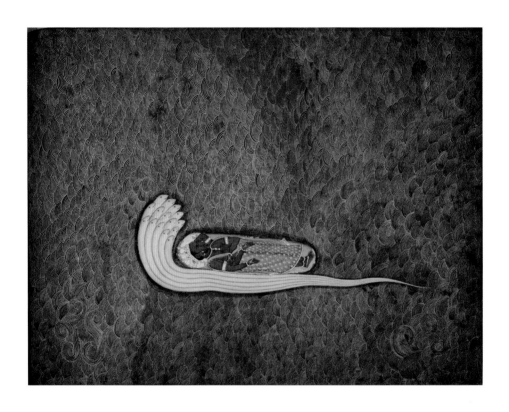

Durga Master, *Reclining Krishna from Sage Markandeya's Ashram and the Milky Ocean*, folio 5 from the Durga Charit Jodphur, *c.* 1780–90.

The milk from a *Lactarius indigo* (Indigo milk mushroom).

The Virgin's blue cloak is bound by costliness. The reason for her blue symbolism is not only mournful, hopeful and celestial, it is economic. In the words of Marina Warner:

> Blue is the colour of space and light and eternity, of the sea and the sky. The reason for the symbolism is also economic, however, for blue was an expensive pigment, obtainable only from crushed lapis lazuli imported from Afghanistan, and after gold, thus became the medieval painter's most fitting tribute to the Queen of Heaven.[31]

In the film *At Five in the Afternoon* (2003), made by the Iranian writer-director Samira Makhmalbaf, set in Afghanistan, the women wear blue burqas in a surreal echo of the famed mines in Afghanistan, which until the nineteenth century were the only known source of lapis lazuli.[32] They wear the blue sky of heaven. The film is a bleak, blue look at poverty, starvation, overcrowding and hope within hopelessness. Makhmalbaf, however, refuses to demonize. The film's title is in reference to Frederico García Lorca's poem in memory of the tragic death of a bullfighter, but the connection remains as oblique as the blue veils of the women. It is a paradox to remember that the lapis lazuli, responsible for so much of the beautiful blues in the paintings of the Virgin, came from Afghanistan. Heaven belongs to nobody. The women of *At Five in the Afternoon* blow through the film, like blue butterflies, shreds of the sky's air,[33] without, by the film's end, any hope of metamorphosis, or even making a sound that could be heard: not even as much as a fly's 'Blue – uncertain stumbling Buzz' (Emily Dickinson).

BLUE EGGS AND INDIGO MUSHROOMS

Blue skin is the colour of death, yet the blue of Vishnu's skin is the optimistic colour of heavenly, infinite life. Here in this

eighteenth-century painting from Jodhpur (the Indian city at
the centre of Rajasthan, which is sometimes called the 'Blue City'
because of the locals' penchant for painting their buildings with
indigo),[34] the Hindu god, Vishnu, is cradled in his multi-headed
serpent vehicle-bed. He is resting on his snaky Shesha. His indigo
face, with 'its pointy chin and sweet, small smile'[35] is comforting.
He is asleep in a silvery ocean of milk. When he awakes, the
whole cycle of creation begins, not unlike the metamorphosis
of the butterfly.

Black and blue make indigo: a colour with a most unpleasant
and violent history. Indeed, 'in 1789 the French colony of Saint-
Domingue (now Haiti and Santo Domingo) had some 1,800 indigo
slave plantations in its western province alone . . . Not sugar [as is
often assumed] but indigo was the chief export for this colony'.[36]
In the words of Michael Taussig, 'Color bequeathed color'.[37]
A paradox riddled with pain.

To make indigo, animal or human urine was used as an
alkali mixed with an already potent smelling vat of crushed
indigo steeped in water. As Taussig notes on the inescapable
seepage of both smell and colour:

> In 17th-century India, indigo workers are reported as wearing
> masks with only the eyes exposed on account of the smell,
> while those close to the work drank milk every hour, 'this being
> a preservative against the subtlety of the indigo'. The workers
> would spit blue for some time after work. An egg placed near
> a person working an indigo vat would, at the end of one day,
> be found to be altogether blue inside . . . Blue food! . . . No
> doubt chemistry can explain this diabolic penetrative power of
> blueness, but can it explain the chill or the unseemly mix of
> metaphors: the masks, the eyes, the blue spit and the blue egg?
> What medley of history and horror, science and poetry, is
> hereby made manifest?[38]

Indigo and milk. The historically venomous combination brings to mind the indigo milkcap (*Lactarius indigo*), one of the few naturally blue foods (unlike the horrid indigo egg, blue inside and out). Like all mushrooms of the *Lactarius* genus, when bruised or scratched, this fungus cries tears of indigo milk. It is difficult to believe that the indigo milk cap is edible, some even say, delicious.

FLYING BLUE

Birds, who live so much of their lives in the sky, can see more depth and variations of blue than other living creatures. Penguins, who fly through the blue ocean, only to pop up and look at the blue sky, must also be able to see underwater with those same eyes, like a fish. It turns out that the penguin (at least the Humboldt Penguin as carefully studied by Graham Martin) has an eye pigment 'sensitive to violet . . . which gives the penguin sensitivity to part of the ultraviolet spectrum, something already demonstrated in the pigeon and hummingbird. But most strikingly the maximum sensitivity of the penguin's pigments are very similar to those of many marine fish'.[39] A penguin can see blues in the air and blues underwater. In New Zealand and Australia there is a species of tiny penguins (*Eudyptula minor*) whose blue skin has given them the name of 'Little Blues'; fittingly, they are also known as 'Fairy Penguins'.

Flying, as has already been fluttered in this text, is blue. The French photographer Bernard Faucon's flying boy 'mannequin' (from the Dutch meaning 'little man') wears blue and soars in a blue sky away from a strange blue pool. (*Faucon* in French means 'falcon'.) The flying doll-boy looks real, as do his mannequin boy-friends, but he is empty, like the photograph itself (which *looks* real but is not). He is empty like the blue sky made of scattered light. Furthermore, this flying butterfly-doll-boy is a creature of

Bernard Faucon, *The Boy Who Flies*, 1976, photograph.

metamorphosis, as is emphasized in the fact that pupa comes from the Latin meaning 'doll', and is also a term for cocoon or chrysalis. Perhaps he is on his way away from childhood itself or to a Neverland where childhood is never lost. Faucon's photograph is entitled *L'Enfant qui vole* (1976), but in French, it also suggests the translation of the child who steals, suggesting something is missing, lost, flying, blue.

Vladimir Nabokov, a famed lepidopterist in his own right, who 'specialized in Blues, a widespread group of small butterflies',[40] describes the pupa of the holometabolous insect with descriptive doll-like language as 'hard and glistening . . . with golden knobs and plate-armour wingcases'.[41] Like adolescence itself, in which something (a caterpillar-like child) hatches into something else (a winged man), 'the pupal stage' can last for a 'few years'.[42] Nabokov remembers 'as a boy keeping a hawkmoth's pupa in a box for something like seven years'.[43] Nabokov notes that he 'actually finished high school while the thing was asleep – and then it finally hatched – unfortunately it happened during a journey on the train'.[44] For Nabokov, the pupa held 'a promise of something wonderful to come': wings and flight, as both a natural scientist and a writer to 'whom metaphors from lepidoptery came easily'[45] (as is evidenced in *Lolita*, his lectures on masterpieces of European fiction, and *The Gift*, *Pnin* and *Speak, Memory*).

Nabokov's small 'Blues' ('mostly a half inch and an inch in wingspread') are not flashy, are not 'the most eye-catching of Lepidoptera': their beauty is 'subtle'.[46] Furthermore, many 'Blues would better be described as brown, copper, gray, silver or even white'.[47] As Nabokov explains, 'when a lepidopterist uses *Blues,* a slangy but handy term for a certain group of Lycaenids, he does not see that word in any color connection because he knows that the diagnostic undersides of their wings are not blue but dun, tan, grayish, etc., and that many Blues, especially in the female, are brown, not blue'.[48] The subtle, flickering blue happens when one spots their upper surfaces. The blue effect of their charming

underwings takes flight in *Pnin*, when 'two characters disturb
a flock of Karner Blues, remarkable butterflies, and now sadly
endangered, that Nabokov himself scientifically named and
described'.[49] From *Pnin*:

> A score of small butterflies, all of one kind, were settled on a
> damp patch of sand, their wings erect and closed, showing
> their pale undersides with dark dots and tiny orange-rimmed
> peacock spots along their hindwing margins; one of Pnin's
> shed rubbers disturbed some of then and revealing the
> celestial hue of their upper surface, they fluttered around
> like blue snowflakes before settling again.[50]

Adam Fuss made his own photogram of a blue butterfly on
a daguerreotype plate. The photogram is a cameraless form of
photography 'made by the contact of an object or objects on
Photographic paper'[51] that is exposed to light. (Later in this book,
photograms made on cyanotype paper will be further addressed.)
The photogram, as first developed in the nineteenth century,
is cheap, is made without a negative and is immediate. The photogram is the Victorian cousin of yesterday's Polaroid and today's
digital image. Yet Fuss then *pins* (one is tempted to say *Pnin's,*
but the pronunciation of the name of Nabokov's character almost
renders the pun mute[52]) *his* butterfly (not on paper) but in the
far less fleeting medium of the complex, 'obsolete historic photographic process' of the daguerreotype. As Martin Barnes explains:

> Daguerreotypes were formed directly on copper plates, which
> were silvered to become photographic, polished like a mirror
> and developed using mercury vapour. Depending on how
> light strikes the plate and the angle from which it is viewed,
> the image flips between negative and positive. Daguerreotypes
> were used from the 1840s until around the 1870s, often as
> *memento mori*, keepsake portraits of deceased loved ones.

The plates were made to be exposed in a camera, and no
photograms on daguerrotype plates from the nineteenth
century have so far been found to exist.[53]

Daguerreotypes, because of their materiality and smallness,
evoke jewellery or special small mirrors and, thereby, emphasize
materiality more than photographs on paper. But Fuss's blue
butterfly is a modern, large daguerreotype (61 × 50.8 cm). His
butterfly flies in a big blue expanse of a mirror of shimmering
blue, the flash and dazzle of the upperside of a Karner Blue writ
large. (The magical iridescent flipping between a positive and
negative image of Fuss's butterfly is impossible to gather in its
reproduction on paper). 'The photogram of the butterfly [by
Fuss] frozen in time mingles with the changing current moment.
It is like seeing the past in the present . . . It is the underlying
tone of sorrow mixed with hope'.[54] Blue, here, is as fleeting as
the process of the photogram (from which it is made): as short
as the life of the flittering butterfly of 'perennial potency'.[55] Blue
here is also as permanent as the process of the daguerreotype
(from which it is made); as eternal as the butterfly (which embraces
the concept of transformation as it moves from caterpillar, to pupa
to winged creature). Blue is as paradoxical as a butterfly. Blue is
a butterfly.

Birds and bugs can see all kinds of blues that we cannot see,
but the price paid, you might say, is to be short-lived. For the
ultraviolet light that their eyes are so attuned to (allowing them,
for example, to see patterns on flowers that are invisible to us)
would create a rate of exposure that would be physically intolerable
to larger, longer-living life. In the words of Simon Ings:

No big animal sees far into the ultraviolet. The larger the eye,
the more light it can take in, and there must be a point at which
the potential damage ultraviolet light can do when focused out-
weighs its usefulness. Many birds and insects have evolved to see

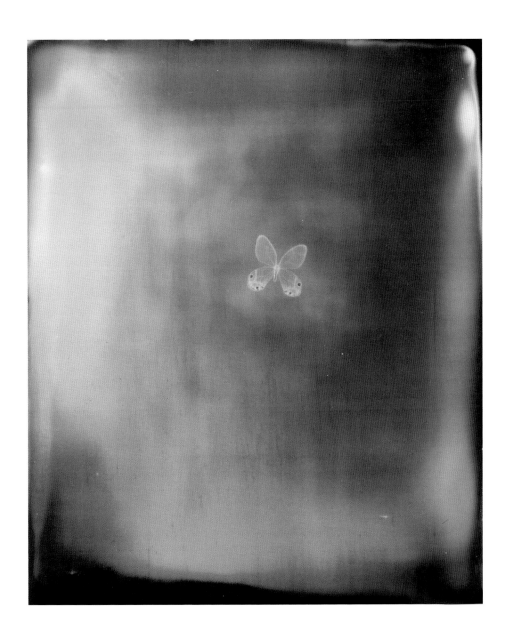

Adam Fuss, *Butterfly Daguerreotype*, from the series *My Ghost*, 2001,
photogram daguerreotype.

ultraviolet wavelength, but they only live for a short time, dying before the damage becomes significant. Large mammals have much longer lives, and their exposure over years could destroy their eyes' photo pigments and turn their lenses cloudy.[56]

Life is short, not only for the minuscule life of the birds and insects who are true connoisseurs of blue, but also for big animals like ourselves who sing the blues. We cannot help but get lost in the blues. Yet, as Padua's canopy of heavenly azure attests to, blue is (Giotto's) joy. Yet blue skin is the sorrowful hue of death. Yet Vishnu's blue skin is heavenly life. Yet joy is when the cyanotic baby takes a big breath and pinkens his blue lips with life. *Blue is joyful-sad.*

3

UNWRAPPING *Blue Boy*

IN 1922, *The Blue Boy* (Thomas Gainsborough's *circa* 1770 portrait
of Jonathan Buttall) left for California, leaving England's National
Gallery. The curator was sad to see the boy go. A favourite.
He scribbled in pencil on the back of one of *The Blue Boy*'s wooden
stretchers, 'Au revoir'. *The Blue Boy* is now proudly displayed at
the Huntington (near Pasadena, California) – across the room
from Thomas Lawrence's portrait of a young girl (Sarah Barrett
Moulton), entitled *Pinkie* (1794). *Pinkie* and *The Blue Boy* were
never meant to be together: it is an arranged marriage that began
when the two were first displayed together at the Huntington in
the 1920s. *Blue Boy* is close to twenty-five years older than *Pinkie*.
From growing up in California, these paintings have long been
familiar to me and they also provide some of the most saccharine
clichés of the colouring of gender and childhood. They satisfy a
cultural desire to underscore the message that blue is for boys
and pink is for girls. I have distaste for *Pinkie*.

But blue can be for girls too. All of this pink for girls is more
of a twentieth-century phenomenon, enhanced and celebrated
by the nuptials at the Huntington. (In defiance of pink is for girls,
one only needs to think of Carlo Collodi's original 1883 *Pinocchio*
and the novel's little girl with blue hair, and her double, the Blue
Fairy, whose name is more accurately translated as the 'Indigo
Fairy'.[1]) Indeed, *Pinkie* and *The Blue Boy* are the favourite specta-
cles of Huntington visitors.

John Gage, one of the great experts on the history of colour
and its meaning, notes some of the twists and turns the gendering
of blue has made since Novalis hued his flower girl blue in 1800:

Blue established its central place in the Romantic imagination
chiefly through the work of the geologist, poet and novelist . . .

Thomas Gainsborough, *The Blue Boy (Jonathan Buttall)*, *c.* 1770, oil on canvas.

who wrote under the name of Noavalis . . . Novalis's novel
Heinrich von Ofterdingen (1800) opens with the hero sleepless
with yearning to see the blue flower . . . Later, he finds himself
in a meadow surrounded by dark-blue rocks under a dark-
blue sky, where he discovers the tall light-blue flower in
whose centre he sees a face. The face turns out to be his
beloved, who when Heinrich meets and dances with her
is revealed to have light sky-blue eyes and blue veins on
her neck. One of Heinrich's chief helpers in this quest is
the shepherd-girl Cyane, whose name derives from the Greek
term for 'blue', and who, in the uncompleted continuation
of the novel, picks the blue flower for him.[2]

Gage gives other examples of other blue girls, noting that
the so-called blueing of girls can be understood as a symbolic
equation of the colour with the feminine power of attraction.
Gage poetically feeds the pull of feminine blue through Goethe,
who would write in his 1810 *Theory of Colours*, 'as we readily
follow an agreeable object that flies from us, so we have to
contemplate blue, not because it advances to us, but because
it draws us after it'.[3]

I am attracted to Gainsborough's *Blue Boy*. He is tied up
with ribbons and blue satin, like a present. His thin satin trousers
stop at the knee and are stylishly tucked into his white stockings.
Each leg is tied with a big golden bow below the knee: the look is
curiously like some of today's Japanese-Lolita-schoolgirl-princess
fashions. *Blue Boy*'s golden shoes sport more big satin bows: blue
with silver trimming.

The image, today, for me, is 'vaguely pornographic . . . naïvely
– or ironically – absorbed in the practice, not of a passivity, but
of an extreme art: that of the package, of *fastening*'.[4] These words
from Roland Barthes were written in a very different context: he is
describing a contemporary photograph of a boy in Japan, but the
concept of the package, with an emphasis on fastening, is very

fitting for the covered-in-bows *Blue Boy*. See, also, Blue Boy's tiny fabric-covered buttons, coupled with silver buttons (like round bells), which fasten his tight jacket. If the painting made sounds, they would be those of a glockenspiel. He rings blue bells. He is a nosegay of bluebells. The costume is seemingly made out of the *cheapness* of *luxurious* satin sheets, thereby echoing the materiality of pornography, of, even, perhaps 'blue films'.

The jacket is trimmed with silver ribbon: it sparkles along the bottom edge of the coat, along up the *fastened* centre and around the splits of the slashed (or paned) sleeves which open up to reveal panels of shimmering white. American college marching bands, with their own penchant for light blue, tassels, sparkle and silver twirling batons come to mind. The collegiate and the pornographic (and, it seems, the eighteenth-century Gainsborough, who here was inspired by the costumes found in the paintings of Anthony van Dyck) all come together.

The satin jacket pulls across his feminine chest, which is narrow with a faint appearance of breasts. Below his navel, the jacket divides to reveal his pre-pubescent tummy, although Buttall is some eighteen years old. Trousers are worn very low on his boyish hips that are pushed out. He stands akimbo. In contemporary terms, this could be read as a 'gay' pose.

There is no *real* interest in what lies beneath the blue satin: instead, the interest is generated by the possibility of unwrapping. 'By its very perfection, this envelope' made out of blue satin suggests an endless unwrapping which 'postpones the discovery of the object it contains'.[5] *Blue Boy* is a guide boy steering us towards the blue that you never arrive at. 'Blue', in the words of Rebecca Solnit (yet again), 'is the color of longing for the distances you never arrive in, for the blue world'.[6]

The huge ostrich feather on his hat is as ludicrous as the big, fluffy, strutting, grounded bird from which it comes. Nevertheless, *Blue Boy* is no ostrich and he draws me after him, like an 'agreeable object' flying away from me (Goethe). He is a shimmering 'Blue' butterfly. A big pointy lace collar frames his face, like little wings, emphasizing his lepidopteran quality. I want to go 'lepping' after him. Pink cheeks, red lips, white skin and black hair turn him into a boyish Snow White. But he is no *Schneewittchen* (German for 'Snow White'); he is a real English blueblood. Gainsborough's *The Blue Boy* is a beautiful, but empty, well-wrapped gift: there for the 'endless unwrapping'.

John Singer Sargent, *The Daughters of Edward Darley Boit*, 1882, oil on canvas.

4
One Cat, Four Girls, Three Blue-and-White Pots: Walpole's 'Selima' and Sargent's *Daughters of Edward Darley Boit*

GIRLS AND BLUE-AND-WHITE POTS

John Singer Sargent's *The Daughters of Edward Darley Boit* (originally exhibited as *Portraits d'enfants*), 1882, features four sisters: four American girls living in Paris. 'Four-year-old Julia sits on the floor'[1] with a pink baby doll painted with the same loose precision Velázquez used for the paint petals of his flower corsage pinned to the Infanta's dress at the heart of *Las Meninas* (1656). The doll is more bouquet than baby and adds to the impression that the four sisters are 'aristocratic flowers' themselves.[2] 'Eight-year-old Mary Louisa stands on the left'[3] in full light; and she is wearing the only dress that is coloured and it is coloured red. 'Jane and Florence, aged twelve and fourteen respectively, stand at the center'.[4] All the girls wear white pinafores shaded in grey and blue-greys, verging at times on light blue, like the carpet upon which Julia sits with childlike frankness. Like the two blue-and-white vases, which stand guard amongst the daughters of Edward Darley Boit, the girls 'seem adrift and alone'.[5]

These vases are huge. They were made in Japan, are extra large, and for decoration only for Western consumers. 'In childhood, objects loom larger than they really are'[6]; in this case, however, the objects of childhood loom even larger than our childish memories and experiences, even larger than the Wedgwood teapot (which has to be blue and white) in Colette and Ravel's *L'enfant et les sortilèges: Fantaisie lyrique en deux parties*. 'The fact that the Boit's vases were transported 'across the ocean more than a dozen times, suffering only relatively minor damage to their rims' is remarkable and excessive.[7] The vases could be understood as displaced (metonymic) vessels of 'home' for their expatriate owners.[8] (The concept of metonymy is further taken up in this book's chapter Ten, 'Like a Stocking').

Currently, the painting is housed at the Boston Museum of Fine Arts, where it is displayed with the original vases: parental sentinels at each side of the painting. *The family is together.*

It is of interest that these four pinafored sisters would never marry. Furthermore, as Erica E. Hirshler tells us, their closest ties would remain amongst the family. *This family is unbreakable.*

> The fragility of the actual vases is evident today in their installation before the painting. The delicate fluting rimming their wide mouths is much mended, and it is obvious that one of the top-heavy vessels would not provide stable support for the full weight of a young woman's body. Florence's near-fusion with this prized possession of her father's is an exaggeration'.[9]

The vase, despite its valiant efforts, could not really support the leaning weight of fourteen-year-old 'Florie'.

I think of objects that have belonged to my grandmother and her father before her. I have a large turtleshell cut-glass vase (alas, not blue) which has bobbed along from Paris to New Zealand to California and, most recently, to England. My big vase and other such carefully transported objects, like the even bigger, gigantic Boit vases, are always, perhaps, *on their way.* I take comfort that the Boit vases and my great-grandfather's vase are not currently subject to *waterways,* yet there is also comfort in knowing that they did and can survive such journeys. Today, my turtleshell glass vase sits with me on my writing desk. Today, the big, blue-and-white Boit vases stand tall in the museum. All is settled, for now.

Of interest is the fact that these displaced Boit vases were
far from empty when they arrived at the museum. Inside them
could be found: 'a cigar stub, a paper airplane, a pink ribbon,
a tennis ball, sheets of geography lessons, a letter about the
repeal of Prohibition, an Arrow shirt collar, an old doughnut,
an admission card to a dance at the Eastern Yacht Club in
Marblehead, Massachusetts, three badminton shuttlecocks,
many coins and a feather'.[10] Without the memories to go with
these objects, they are not souvenirs. They are tokens of loss;
rubbish swallowed by these blue-and-white curvaceous figures
with thin necks, and, like the daughters of Edward Darley Boit,
they have nothing to say.

A CAT AND A BLUE-AND-WHITE POT

Horace Walpole was an eighteenth-century collector, historian and
writer who invented the word '*gloomth*' to go with his aesthetic,
fabulously constructed little 'mock-Gothic', 'mock-castle', 'Gothic
mousetrap', 'confection', 'gingerbread castle', 'paper house', 'play-
ground of affectation'[11] called Strawberry Hill. It all began in 1747,
when 'Walpole leased a nondescript suburban house (built in
1698) from Mrs. Chevenix, a famous seller in trinkets'.[12] Walpole
described the acquisition of the little house (which is 'palatial' in
'modern terms' but 'dinky' by the 'standards of Georgian magnifi-
cence') as getting a little 'plaything . . . out of Mrs Chevenix's
shop and is the prettiest bauble you ever saw'.[13] It did not take
Walpole long to fill his wee castle with enough art, relics and
curios to make it perfectly modern Gothic, perfectly 'gloomth'.
In 1754 ('amongst four thousand *surviving* letters'[14]), Walpole
wrote, Strawberry 'is now in the height of its greenth, blueth,
honeysuckle, and seringahood'.[15] Likewise, in a letter of 1753,
Walpole wrote: 'One has a satisfaction in imprinting the gloomth
of abbeys and cathedrals on one's house'.[16]

In addition to his attraction to and aesthetic development of 'gloomth',[17] Walpole inherited 'the taste for pets'[18] from his parents. Amongst these pets was a favourite cat named Selima. The cat was fascinated by the goldfish that the eccentric Walpole kept inside his large blue-and-white-porcelain Chinese tub (*c.* 1730). 'Goldfish were a relatively recent craze'.[19] 'The pattern on the tub is known as "the Three Friends of Winter." The pine tree stands for venerable old age, the bamboo for bravery and strength of character (it may bend but never break), and the prunus for youth, beauty and the first appearance of spring.'[20] In February of 1747, Selima drowned in the large Chinese blue-and-white tub. She liked to 'perch on its edge, fascinated by the glittering movement of the goldfish within'.[21] (It may have been hunger for the fish or the pleasure of the catch, but perhaps there was also a bit of feline Gothic Narcissus or dark-dramatic Ophelia at play.) Thomas Gray, a friend of Walpole, wrote a detached, amused and ironic poem in honour of the cat that was eventually even illustrated (1797–98) by William Blake. It begins like this:

ODE On the Death of a Favourite CAT,
Drowned in a Tub of Gold Fishes

'TWAS on a lofty vase's side,
Where China's gayest art had dy'd
The azure flowers, that blow;
Demurest of the tabby kind,
The pensive Selima reclin'd,
Gazed on the lake below.[22]

A special pedestal was made for the tub. On the pedestal's label was written the first stanza of the poem, making a bit of witty 'gloomth' for all the fancy visitors to see as they walked into the 'Great Cloister at Strawberry Hill'.[23] Later, the blue-and-white Chinese tub, along with the pedestal displaying the first stanza of

Gray's Ode, was moved to 'ceremonial pride of place in the Little Cloister' of Strawberry Hill, making it 'one of the most prominently displayed *objets d'art* that visitors would encounter in the lobby, to the right of the entrance of the house'.[24] Blue loss is not always so serious. It can be 'gloomth'.

In both cases (Sargent's *The Daughters of Edward Darley Boit* and Horace Walpole's Strawberry Hill theatrics with Selima), oversized blue-and-white pots, two from nineteenth-century Japan, one from eighteenth-century China, are childish, upper-crust, fairy-tale stuff. Pots big enough, if you are small enough (whether child or cat), to crawl inside. Inside the Japanese vases there reside tokens of lost childhood play. Inside the Chinese tub there resides play itself, that is childish, foppish and mawkish. All three are vessels for keeping the blues of childhood and childish play under their lips of their lidless, Pandora-like jars.

Horace Walpole's Goldfish Tub, *c.* 1730, Chinese porcelain tub.

5
'A THING OF BLUE BEAUTY IS A GUILT FOR EVER'

BLUES ARE MINUSCULE mournful knots of ink condensed, saved, savoured and rationed in a letter by Irène Némirovsky (that we now know as *Suite Française*), which documents evils of the Vichy Regime. Her daughter Denise did not know that the journal was a manuscript for a book; she thought it was a painful private diary. As a Jewish girl in hiding, on the run with her sister and governess, she had been told to hide her nose, was given a false name and was given the choice of taking her doll or the manuscript. The doll was left behind. But it was years before she could open the book: she was unable to bear her mother's words of 'just-before' (just-before the arrest, just-before Auschwitz). So the fat book filled with blue was stashed away in its suitcase, darkly hidden. For a long time, the tiny heartbeats of blue remained unheard. It was not until Denise's Paris house was flooded that the suitcase was opened. Némirovsky's tangled blue knots of letters were nearly drowned. But luckily, under a magnifying glass, they were brought to rhyming in the light. It took twenty years. Némirovsky's story (written in the smallest possible script to save ink, which was as precious as that wartime's sugar and milk, on carefully rationed paper) was not a journal: it spoke a novel. M-O-U-R-N-I-N-G glory. ('She placed a creamy earthenware jug of forget-me-nots on the table'.[1]) Between its pages Némirovsky tellingly misquotes Keats's 1818 poem 'Endymion', writing *not* that 'A thing of beauty is a joy for ever'– but rather, 'A thing of beauty is a guilt for ever'.[2] The book's English translator did not correct this error: this *blue* mistake is a poignant reminder that the book was 'written in the depths of the French countryside, with a sense of urgent foreboding and nothing but her memory as a source.'[3]

Blue is for victory: the Nazis did not truly succeed in killing Irène Némirovsky.

Irène Némirovsky, 'Suite Française' in the Manuscrit d'Irène Némirovsky, c. 1941,
ink on paper.

6
MILK AND SUGAR ARE BLUE

IN TONI MORRISON'S 1970 wounding novel (set in Ohio in the grim year of 1941, near the beginning of the USA's entry into the Second World War), entitled *The Bluest Eye,* there is a little black girl named Pecola whose name sounds dark and dirty like coal, but also sweet and syrupy like Coca-Cola. Pecola gulps down glasses of milk in a Shirley Temple-blue, Depression-era, glass cup. She wants blue eyes and the milky whiteness that they represent more than anything in the world, and even consumes *'three* quarts of milk' in one sitting, just to take advantage of using the Shirley Temple cup that obsessed her.[1] The cup is clear blue, like a fantasy of the little starlet's glass-blue eyes. The outcome is violent for this African violet. A catastrophe.

Milk, which is a totem drink for Americans, like tea is for the British, like wine is for the French, can be calm and restorative, as Barthes notes of the dense, creamy substance in his *Mythologies.* Milk, as Pecola's desire testifies and as Barthes' words highlight is also 'cosmetic'.[2] As Barthes argues, '[m]oreover, its purity, associated with the innocence of the child, is a token of strength . . . the equal of reality'.[3] But in *The Bluest Eye* these endless cups of milk are bankrupt for Pecola. She lives in a culture that force-feeds her the *reality* of 'whiteness'. Rather than fighting, she is held by the psychological, atrocious, force-feeding instrument of dominant culture. She gives in, like a goose being fattened with figs, to produce hypertrophied livers. The world eats her up, despite her efforts to eat otherwise. She is not able to float on her milky ocean, unlike indigo Krishna sleeping on his snaky Sheba boat.[4] Pecola takes metaphor for milky 'reality' and eats whiteness, in order 'to enter into intercourse with it'.[5] This milk turns blue with violence, as if oozing from a bruised *Lactarius indigo* mushroom. In French, *bleu* means both the colour and a bruise.

Sugar tells us a similar gastro-racist story in *The Bluest Eye*. Just as Pecola loves to drink her milk in a Shirley Temple blue cup, she also loves to eat sugary Mary Jane candies (sweets with the taste of molasses and peanut butter, not unlike a Peanut Butter Kiss or a Squirrel Nut Zipper or a Bit-O-Honey) packaged in their own blue-eyed girl yellow wrappers ('the yellow tint of a faded bruise'[6]):

> each pale yellow wrapper has a picture on it. A picture of little Mary Jane, for whom the candy is named. Smiling white face. Blond hair in gentle disarray, blue eyes looking at her out of a world of clean comfort. The eyes are petulant, mischievous. To Pecola they are simply pretty. She eats the candy, and its sweetness is good. To eat the candy is somehow to eat the eyes, eat Mary Jane. Love Mary Jane. Be Mary Jane.

Three pennies had brought her nine lovely orgasms with Mary Jane.[7]

Sugar, like milk, is not innocent or even mild, it is rife with *violence,* like a photograph that *shoots,* kills a moment in time, overfills our sight, replaces memory with tangible pictures. As Barthes writes in *Camera Lucida*:

> The Photograph is violent: not because it shows violent things, but because on each occasion *it fills the sight by force*, and because in it nothing can be refused or transformed so that we can sometimes call it mild does not contradict its violence: many say that sugar is mild, *but to me sugar is violent*, and I call it so.[8]

In the vast collection of London's British Museum is a deep blue glass sugar bowl with these words in gilt: 'EAST INDIA SUGAR not made by SLAVES'. (Echoed here are the misquoted words of Keats by Irène Némirovsky: 'A thing of Beauty is a guilt for ever'.⁹) The bowl encouraged the boycotting of sugar from West Indian slave plantations. The anti-slavery sugar bowl (made out of the famous blue glass from Bristol, *circa* 1800–1830) shares the materiality of clear, cobalt blue glass with the Shirley Temple cup. In both, the irises of blue eyes are coloured by the black pupils: holes for light.

7

TIMBER, TIMBRE: *Hearing Blue Again*

ROLAND BARTHES, ALWAYS old-fashioned, appealingly out-of-date, describes the warm sound of wooden toys as follows: 'when the child handles and knocks it, it neither vibrates nor grates, it has a sound at once muffled and sharp. It is a familiar and poetic substance, which does not sever the child from close contact with the tree'.[1]

In Giotto's *Christ Entering Jerusalem* in the Arena Chapel, a figure, young and androgynous in appearance, dressed in a pale pink robe, has climbed a tree for a better look. In close contact with the tree, he seems to be listening, as his almond eyes take in the scene. A blue hum. A rustle.

The *Oxford English Dictionary* defines *timbre* as a 'sonorous quality of any instrument or of a voice'. In Giotto's tree, bent into an image of listening, the timbre is a murmur of leaves. (A 'blue' note is a bent note.) Similarly, the strange still trees of Giotto's *Joachim Among the Shepherds* (also in the Arena Chapel) create the sound of silence. Balled-up leaves are bound by the bold blue of the sky around them.

Black British artist Chris Ofili has made his own blue trees, snakes, ladies, men and grapes for his darkly invested body of paintings and sculptures entitled *Blue Rider* (2005). A corresponding blue-and-silver dual-language book (German-English) was published on the occasion of Ofili's *Blue Rider* exhibition at Contemporary Fine Arts, Berlin.[2] In this work, Ofili 'riffs' on the famous publication made by Wassily Kandinsky and Franz Marc. (The latter famously publishing their *Blue Rider* text in 1912.) Ofili's book is full of sound, not only the *blues* of his painting and sculptures, but also the inclusion of a poem written by the spoken word artist Louis Antwi (*Tru Deep*), appropriately entitled 'Blue and Silva'.[3] Likewise, Greg Tate (writer, guitarist and founder of

Giotto, *Entry into Jerusalem* (detail), Arena Chapel, Padua.

Giotto, *Joachim Entering the Wilderness* (detail), Arena Chapel, Padua.

the improvisational band 'Burnt Sugar') has provided a bluesy, rapping, spiritual in his spoken song / essay, entitled 'Negro Heaven (Blues Clues)'. In German the title is *'Negerhimmel (Blues Clues)'*, giving it a very different timbre.[4]

A tree is a source of *timber*, which produces the *timbre* of the violin, the cello, the viola da gamba.

In *Blue Sparrow*, a painting from Ofili's *Blue Rider* series, a black woman with blue hair, blue skin, blue full lips, below a silver moon, is singing (is smoking) blue dreams. Everything is black, blue and silver, through Ofili's use of gouache, charcoal, ink and aluminium leaf. The woman, whose name is presumed to be 'Blue Sparrow', lies behind heavy, parted curtains. From her mouth a tree of silver *choral* sprouts. Silver notes boogie-woogie to the song. Two blue pyramids in an echo of her blue breasts provide the Egyptian-blue landscape behind her. A single bunch of grapes, like silver coins on a stem, bob and bop along with the blue notes. The silver grapes dangle over the shoulder of another, nearly hidden, figure, who is at one with the curtains. She, or he, has a dusky body with two silver eyes and a silver mouth. He, or she, is dank, sexy, scary, happy, snaky and liquidy. The smoking Blue Sparrow has silver fingernails and a silver cigarette. She has a single, silver Egyptian eye: no pupil. Blue and silver, this chirping odalisque resonates with Antwi's 'Blu and Silva'. Here is a sample:

> Dropping silver sentences like copper,
> Except one,
> Which she placed carefully, as if uncertain,
> in those silver entwined presentation boxes
> she called eyes.
>
> Eyes that exhaled words.
> . . .
> My blue bottle mind busked for copper words to match

Chris Ofili, *Blue Sparrow*, 2005, charcoal, gouache, ink, aluminium on paper.

her silver tongue.
Searched for crevices of sound.[5]

The sound is as important as the message. In French, *timbre* means stamp. Yves Klein just happened to make his own blue *timbre*. ('In 1957, Klein proclaimed the advent of the "Blue Epoch"',[6] sending out invitations to two Paris exhibitions with an original *timbre bleu.*) Homonyms (and near homonyms) give me joy. They open up what Jean-Luc Nancy calls 'listening to the beyond-meaning'.[7]

Jouissance resonates with *j'ouïs sens* ('I heard meaning'). A prime example of this 'listening to the beyond meaning'.[8] 'Listening to the beyond meaning' is a way to cut open myths, in order to make new ones. Blue is the perfect colour for listening beyond meaning.

'Excuse me while I kiss the sky'.[9]

Excuse me while I kiss the 'Negerhimmel'.

8
A BOLT FROM THE BLUE

À ma fille Aline, ce cahier est dédié.
Notes éparses, sans suite comme les rêves, comme la vie toute
faite de morceaux.

For my daughter Aline, this notebook is dedicated.
Scattered notes, like dreams without continuity, like life
made of pieces.

Paul Gauguin, *Cahier pour Aline*, 1893

WHEN AN ISLAND rises out of the Prussian blue sea, it is making
a dream. An island is a bed in the sea, a hatchery for dreams, an
invitation to daydreams of refuge.[1] Paul Gauguin (1848–1903)
accepted this invitation, sailed away and painted his dreams
through a lens that was often blue.

Dreams are a form of pilgrimage. Dreams are a form of travel.
A bed can be a boat. Without leaving home, beds can take us
somewhere else. 'Because I know that time is always time / And
place is always and only place' (T. S. Eliot, 'Ash Wednesday'),
dreaming affords contact with, not only a *geographic other*, but
also an *other time*. I fall into the bed of dreams that stir from
Gauguin's 1892 *Manao Tupapau* (*Spirit of the Dead Watching*).
I fall into the bed of dreams that stir from Gauguin's 1881 *La Petite
rêve* (*Little Girl Dreaming*, 1881).

With a nod from Joan Miró's 1925 abstract *Photo: Ceci est
la couleur de mes rêves* (*Photo: This is the Colour of my Dreams*),
where underneath his little island of thick azure paint he has
written in lovely black script '*Ceci est la couleur de mes rêves*'
('this is the colour of my dreams'), I begin a dream of blue. I make
blue reveries in the darkness of my mind. Like little travelogues,

65

Joan Miró, *This is the Colour of My Dreams*, 1925, oil and pencil on canvas.

these dreams come in bursts and spurts, from the indigo-blackness of my imagination. They come like films by the Lumière brothers lasting fifty seconds.

According to Michael Balint, such flights of fancy escape, both real and imagined, are centred on a fantasy of the return to the Motherland: 'Flying dreams and the oceanic feeling are to be regarded as repetition either of the very early mother-child relationship or of the still earlier intra-uterine existence, during which we were really one with our universe and were really floating in the amniotic fluid with practically no weight to carry'.[2] In this claim, Balint is making use of Freud's famed notion of the oceanic (*Civilization and Its Discontents*, 1930): 'a sensation of "*eternity*", a feeling as of something limitless, unbounded – as it were, "oceanic"'.[3] This *oceanic* feeling, Freud argues, *travels back home*, returns to early childhood experiences. Likewise, according to Freud, the oceanic is associated with personal mysticism and spirituality.[4] Gauguin's voyages home (whether geographic, temporal, spiritual or artistic) were always exotic, even while living in France. They were tirelessly *oceanic*. As Gauguin concludes, after explaining some of the whys and wherefores of *Spirit of the Dead Watching*: 'Otherwise it is simply a study of an Oceanian nude' (*Cahier pour Aline*).[5]

In 1881, many years before Miró's blue dream, Gauguin painted his own blue painting of his dreaming daughter, his treasured Aline, asleep: *La Petite rêve* (*Little Girl Dreaming*). Later in life, Gauguin would refer to this painting as *Sweet Dreams*.[6] Aline, Gauguin's favourite of his five children from his Danish wife Mette, is age three and one half.[7] Gauguin will later set sail for the South Seas, leaving behind Aline, her mother and her siblings. Aline will die young, still a child really, of pneumonia at age nineteen. The story is unhappy. Nevertheless, Gauguin will not let go of her, even after death. Writing in 1897 from Tahiti to Mette: 'Her [Aline's] tomb over there, the flowers, that's all pretence. Her tomb is here beside me; my tears are living flowers'.[8]

In *La Petite rêve*, Aline's blousy nightshirt is a sail of grey-blue,
baby blue, dappled violet-blue. With her feathery hair mysteriously
shorn, like the fuzzy head of a baby bird (she suffered from hair
loss throughout her young life), she rests in her black-iron bed
that snuggles her, as if in a nest. The shadowy black wainscoting
that holds her bed's cloud of white bedclothes further bowers her,
the latter speckled with Monet-like reflections of light-filled greens,
transparent lavender and sky blues. In the corner of the painting
a bearded clown figure, perhaps a doll, wears a red Harlequin
jacket with brass buttons, a blue-and-yellow-striped hat and blue
trousers. The doll-man, helpless with no hands, beckons us into
the dreamscape he shares with the girl. The clown is curiously
reminiscent of Gauguin and might be read as a portrait of the
artist himself, not unlike Manet as Polichenelle (or Pierrot) in the
corner of his 1873 *Masked Ball*.[9] (*Alline* is my mother's middle
name. I drift in a blue dream, between time and place. Between
Aline with one 'l' and Alline with two 'l's.)

Carried away by the clouds of her bed, the dreams in her head,
Aline's bed is her boat. She is a little girl Krishna, floating in
her own ocean of milk. In line with the turned-away gaze of the
dreaming girl's unseen closed eyes, is the 'evocative motif of a bird
taking flight'[10] from a field of wistful greens. Aline is pictured as
seeing a vision, as if reiterating her father's emphasis on 'inner
vision', of seeing with one's eyes closed.[11] Closed off from the
world, but alive in her dreams, Aline is also in tune with Gauguin's
intriguing 1889 ceramic *Jug in the form of a head, self-portrait*
('the pathos of his tortured features, shaped to suggest an ancient
Peruvian portrait vase'[12]), where not only are the artist's eyes
closed, but his ears are cut off too, making him a blind and deaf
island unto the world, with sight and sound only in the imagination, in dreams.

Many years after documenting Aline asleep and dreaming of
flight in unreal colour, Gauguin painted his famed *Manao Tupapau*
(*Spirit of the Dead Watching*), which features his child-bride,

Paul Gauguin, *Little Girl Dreaming*, 1881, oil on canvas.

the thirteen-year-old Tahitian girl named Tehamana. The very
opposite of *Little Girl Dreaming,* Tehamana with her dark skin
and long black hair is naked. She lies on her belly, with the full
taut flesh of adolescent youth, and eyes the viewer the way
that young girls still do today: unabashedly, full of fear and
confidence. The colours of this painting are juicy, tropical, wild
and gastronomically infused: purples, blues, guava juice pink,
cocoa browns, butter creams and liquorice blacks. A particularly
vivid yellow mango colours the floral print that jumps out from
the indigo linen upon which Tehamana lies. A black spirit
figure, primitively painted with a single Egyptian eye, watches
over the scene. With her eyes wide open, Tehamana is seeing
a vision. Or the spirit is seeing her. (As Gauguin writes in his
journal for Aline: 'The title *Manao Tupapau* has two meanings,
either the girl thinks of the spirit, or the spirit thinks of her'.[13])
The purple and blue background is meant to depict the 'phospho-
rescent flowers of the *tupapau* . . . the signs that the spirit nears
you'.[14]

Gauguin's 'spirit of the dead' echoes the partially hidden
figure in Ofili's *Blue Sparrow.* Gauguin, if without the Ofili irony,
finds music in his painting. As Gauguin writes of the *Spirit of the
Dead Watching* in the small notebook for his daughter, 'To sum
up: The musical part; undulating horizontal lines; harmonies of
orange and blue, united by the yellows and purples (their deriva-
tives) lit by greenish sparks'.[15]

Gauguin's remarks on *Manao Tupapau* in *Cahier pour Aline*
make a link between the dreaming sky-blue bed-boat of toddler-
girl Aline with the dreaming (or dreamed) indigo-ocean bed-boat
of adolescent-girl Tehamana. 'In many respects', as Charles
Stuckey remarks, *Spirit of the Dead Watching* is 'a reworking of
Sweet Dreams [Little Girl Dreaming]'.[16] Two children, two times,
two places collide, with an erotic (yet tender) what? Is the Tahitian
painting, through the lens of snow-white-blue Aline, an effort to
coincide lost times and lost places?

The child is indisputably part of Gauguin's 'primitive' repertoire.[17] Gauguin's compelling and problematic nostalgia for childhood is the blue thought that links his early, innocent *Little Girl Dreaming / Sweet Dreams* with his late, erogenous *Spirit of the Dead Watching*; one plays at loss with a blackbird ready to take off, one boldly gives loss the face of strange figure, cloaked in indigo black.

According to the 1919 novel by W. Somerset Maugham, based on the life of the painter, entitled *The Moon and Sixpence*, Gauguin was motivated by a 'divine nostalgia'.[18] While the Greek root of the word nostalgia, *nostos*, means 'the return home'– anyone who has been there knows that the return home is never without pain. Nostalgia feels like getting the blues. According to the *Oxford English Dictionary*, 'nostalgia' is 'a form of melancholia caused by prolonged absence from one's home or country; severe homesickness'. Indeed, 'Nostos might hold out that promise that, yes, you can return whence you came, but nostalgia happens because you can't go home again'.[19] You cannot be a child again. As the narrator of *The Moon and Sixpence* says to the character we recognize as Gauguin, 'I see you as the eternal pilgrim to some shrine that perhaps does not exist. I do not know to what inscrutable Nirvana you aim'.[20]

When I think of Gauguin, I think of elsewhere: 'Because I know that time is always time / And place is always and only place'. Gauguin sailed through life far from my own. How quickly the past becomes remote: the blue. The light that got lost.

The colour blue is made up of the light that got lost. We have already taken pleasure in lines from Rebecca Solnit's *Field Guide to Getting Lost*, in which she notes that 'the world is blue at its edges and in its depths' and that 'blue is the color of longing for the distances you never arrive in, for the blue world'. Here in full is the passage from which these astute lines derive:

The world is blue at its edges and in its depths. This blue is the light that got lost. Light at the blue end of the spectrum does not travel the whole distance from the sun to us. It disperses among the molecules of the air, it scatters in water. Water is colorless, shallow water appears to be the color of whatever lies underneath it, but deep water is full of this scattered light, the purer the water the deeper the blue. The sky is blue for the same reason, but the blue at the horizon, the blue of the land that seems to be dissolving into the sky, is a deeper, dreamier, melancholy blue, the blue at the farthest reaches of the places where you see for miles, the blue of distance. This light that does not touch us, does not travel the whole distance, the light that gets lost.[21]

Yet, the more I dream of Gauguin, the closer he gets. I look at Gauguin's Aline and I think of my mother, Dorothy Alline and 'I stare intensely at the Sovereign Good of childhood . . . of the mother-as-child'.[22] Yet it is more than seeing the two Al(l)ines. It is more than Gauguin's *Sweet Dreams* through the name of and the luminosity of my mother's blue-green eyes.[23] Lost blue light begins to, 'utopically', travel towards me through the grey-blue eyes of my great-grandfather.

My great-grandfather Edward was a real traveller – he sped by boat all around the world, including journeys to France, but also to Australia, San Francisco, Hong Kong, New Caledonia, Japan, Canada, Tahiti and California. It is quite possible, perhaps even likely, that Gauguin may have passed my great-grandpa Edward on the streets in Papeete (Tahiti), if not Sydney (Australia), Paris (France), or Auckland (New Zealand). Contact between my great, great-Grandpa and that self-claimed savage Gauguin would be quite a novel.

Contact seems even more likely with the knowledge that it was in 1895, from 19 August to 29 August, when, on his way back to Tahiti, Gauguin found himself stuck for a full ten days at the Albert Hotel on Queen Street in Auckland. Back then, and still today, Auckland is centred on Queen Street. The daughter of Edward Seering Matthews, my great-aunt Lorna had even been born by then. Could Gauguin have shot Lorna a loving, paternal look in memory of his own, then abandoned, Aline? If Gauguin saw Lorna asleep and cradled in the arms of her father, perhaps he dreamed of his own Aline dreaming?

In all of those art history classes of my youth the past seemed so far away, so foreign. I could never have imagined any contact between Gauguin and a relative I knew and whom I loved, that is, great-aunt Lorna. Perhaps, then, in contradiction to David Lowenthal's 1985 book *The Past is a Foreign Country*, the past is *not* a foreign country: the past may not be as distant as we might have first thought.[24]

Edward Seering Matthews and his daughter (who would grow up, marry and become Lorna Starr), and the painter Paul Gauguin (a being so foreign to my lived life) each traced maps, it seems, onto a possible shared terrain. Such contact is miniscule. But it hits me with its own *punctum*-like force. (*Punctum* is the name that Barthes gives to a tiny detail in a photograph, a 'sting, speck, cut, little hole', which 'shoots out' and 'pierces' him 'like an arrow'.[25]) I feel *punctum* when looking at old photographs of not only my New Zealand relatives, but also at old photographs of Gauguin. I feel a shudder. I hear 'the tiny sound of my shutter falling – that little trapdoor catching light, opening and closing like valves of the heart'.[26] I am touched, as Barthes would say, by 'the delayed rays of a star'.[27] (The delayed rays of Lorna Starr touch me.) I feel surprise. In my thesaurus under 'surprise', I find 'bolt from the blue'.

9
Semioclasm Cyanoclasm

IN ALL FORMS of writing (literary, theoretical, scientific and especially historical), Hayden White emphasizes the style in which a text is written as a driving force of its content. White insists that we think about the content of the form, especially in the work of historical writing. Part of White's project is to expose the literary dimensions of history. White renders all 'voice' as method, including *supposed* disinterested neutrality. Similarly, Roland Barthes' *Mythologies* releases 'myth', with a like-minded attention to form as content.[1] Through a close study of 'the sign' of 1950s French bourgeois culture, Barthes performs what he refers to, in the 1970 preface to *Mythologies*, as *semioclasm* (semiotics + iconoclasm).[2] Both White and Barthes are *semioclastic* rhetoricians.[3]

SEMIOCLASM

The following are examples of Barthes' *semioclasm* at work in *Mythologies*. In 'Toys', '[c]urrent toys [. . .] moulded out of plastic, are at once gross and hygienic'; and 'their very material introduces one to a coenaethesis of use, not pleasure'.[4] Faced with dolls who wet their nappies, miniature medical kits and other objects which constitute a socialized modern adult life – 'the Army, Broadcasting, the Post Office'[5] – children are prepared to be 'users, not creators'. Such toys fail at fostering discovery.

In 'The *Blue Guide*', Barthes' analysis of the Hachette World Guides (dubbed *Le Guide bleu* in French)[6] finds that all scenery is depicted as impossibly '*picturesque*'.[7] In Barthes' short case study of the *Guide*'s treatment of Spain, we go on a *sightless* tour. For the *Blue Guide* does not want us to see poverty, dirt, class struggle, race, or even history. The *Blue Guide* shows us Spain through a series of monuments without history ('it is well known that History is not a good bourgeois'[8]). In the hands of the *Blue Guide*,

> the ethnic reality of Spain is . . . reduced to a vast classical ballet, a nice neat commedia dell'arte, whose improbable typology serves to mask the real spectacle of conditions, classes and professions. For the *Blue Guide*, men exist as social entities only in trains, where they fill a 'very mixed' [picturesque] Third Class.[9]

As Barthes makes clear, 'The *Guide* becomes, through an operation common to all mystifications, the very opposite of what it advertises, an agent of blindness'.[10]

In 'Wine and Milk', the French enjoy the warmness of wine without thinking about the fact that the grapes were grown mostly by Muslims in Algeria, that is, by people who have been oppressed and colonized by the French, people whose religion forbids them to drink.

In 'Ornamental Cookery', the smoothness of richly illustrated recipes in women's magazines are set up for consuming with the eyes, not the mouth. These colourful empty pictures are all glaze.

In 'Steak and Chips', Barthes finds that steak in France is nationalized like wine. *Bifsteck frites* are extra French, adding even more 'national glamour'.[11] For 'chips are nostalgic and patriotic like steak'. But steak is also believed to hold strength-giving blood. This makes steak at once (French) 'Culture' and (life-giving) 'Nature'. The sanguineness of the steak must thereby be fully respected. Overcooking a steak is morally offensive. Cooking steak past rare, even moderately, is pushing the limit of both nationhood and morality. The 'prestige of steak evidently derives from its quasi-rawness . . . Full-bloodedness is the raison d'être of steak . . . rare steak is said to be *saignant . . .* or *bleu*'.[12]

In the 'The New Citroën', the Citroën breaks through as the new Gothic Cathedral. It is an 'exaltation of glass'.[13] Indeed, '[t]he glass surfaces are not windows, openings pieced in a dark shell, they are vast walls of air and space . . . originating from the heaven of *Metropolis*'.[14] The new Citroën is a new goddess, who just happens to be called the *Déesse* or the *D.S.* 19.[15] She is 'mediatized' through 'exorcism' in the exhibition hall, she is the 'very essence of petit-bourgeois advancement'.[16] *You can have her* in blue.

By borrowing the riggings of Barthes, *Blue Mythologies* sets sail on a *cyanoclastic* tour.

10

LIKE A STOCKING: *Two Paths of Metaphor and Metonymy*

METAPHOR

One path of *Blue Mythologies* is blue *as metaphor*.[1]

Marcel Proust is no foreigner to metaphor. Proust's *In Search of Lost Time* has a particular penchant for metaphors hued blue. *The Captive* (volume v of the *Search*) is smitten with blue. There, we join 'Marcel'[2] in his quest for the enigmatic, captivating, watery Albertine, but she is impossible for him to capture. She slips through his fingers like water. Albertine is (metaphorically) the sea. It is all in her seaside irises. As Proust writes:

> Her blue, almond-shaped eyes, grown longer, had not kept their form; they were indeed the same colour, but seemed to have passed into a liquid state. So much so that, when she shut them it was as though a pair of curtains had been drawn to shut out a view of the sea.[3]

'Metaphor', as the great *tropologist* Hayden White explains, 'means something like "anything that has to do with similarity"'.[4] Like the ocean spilling out of Albertine's eyes (or like pulling a stocking over a shapely leg), metaphor is expansion.

METONYMY

The other path of *Blue Mythologies* is blue as *metonymy*. 'Metonymy', White tells us, 'means "anything that has to do with contiguity"'.[5] In Krzysztof Kieślowski's 1993 film, *Blue*, a mother named Julie loses her daughter Anna in a car accident. After Julie's loss, this grieving mother finds a blue lollipop in her handbag. She had saved it for her daughter. The saved, sacrosanct sucker, in the shape of a tongue coloured blue, is the exact 'sweet' that Anna had been eating at the time of the accident. Anna is metonymically the blue lolly.[6] Like a favourite sweet without the child (or like a stocking that retains the shape of the leg that no longer wears it), metonymy is displacement.

METAPHORIC-METONYMIC

Nevertheless, the expansion of the metaphor and the displacement of the metonymy turn on one another, like a stocking turning inside out and right side out. Far from opposites, metaphor and metonymy are, in fact, friendly in touch; they are inversions of one another. As White has rightly pointed out, 'metaphor and metonymy have to be understood in contemporary discourse as metaphors'.[7] Similarly, Julia Kristeva turns to word compounding and draws attention to the non-differentiation of the differences between metaphor and metonymy as 'metaphorico-metonymic'.[8]

At the start of Proust's *Search* – a novel about trying to write a novel, a journey into writing – Marcel is mystified by the two walks near his boyhood summer home in Combray, these are the Méséglise way and the Guermantes way. By the end of the novel, Marcel learns that the two ways are linked and are one in the same course, like metaphor (philosophy) and metonymy (novel). These two paths are a *mise en abyme* of approaches (geographic and rhetorical). They are the 'metaphorico-metonymic' waves of the back and forth motion of *Blue Mythologies.*

A BLUE STOCKING

As children, many of us had the satisfaction of making simple cyanotypes (camera-less photographs). We took sheets of rich blue, light-sensitive paper out into the bright sun and placed objects directly on the paper. Perhaps these were a hat, a sock, a flower or an Ophelia wreath of leaves. Then we waited for the blue paper to turn almost white in the sunlight. This took about five to seven minutes depending on the brightness of the day. Next, in the kitchen sink, or the bathtub, we *developed* the image under water. While watching the blue fade and then reappear like the sped-up film of a changing sky, we saw the exquisite 'white negative' of the chosen object magically appear.

Annabel Dover uses the same process: she places a hat, a sock, a flower, an Ophelia wreath of leaves or a stocking on the cyanotype paper. Dover's 'stocking' is not only useful as an image of the colour blue as expanding metaphor and displacing metonymy, it also wittily plays into depths of the negative-positive paradox of the term 'bluestocking'. The label of 'bluestocking' was first used to designate an intellect of both sexes. After the eighteenth century, 'bluestocking' referred only to the learned of the gentler sex. As time went by, the female pedant became known as a 'bluestocking'. This developed as a negative description for smart women, who, because of their superior intellect, must also be frumpy, preferring worsted blue stockings to silky ones. A 'bluestocking' is a positive that turns into a negative.

Dover's blue stocking is certainly silky: its transparency makes for the beauty of the cyanotype. The 'negative' of the solid black seam is a delicious positive serpentine white, like piping on cake. The stocking belonged to the artist's grandmother who stored and kept her sheer and sexy stockings, with their scrumptious seams for running up the back of legs, in anticipation of her husband's return from the Second World War.

But the husband went *missing*. He never returned. He was presumed dead.

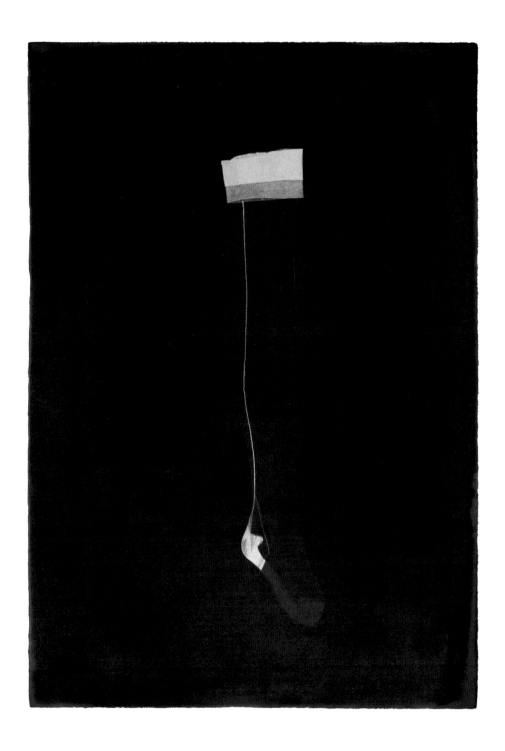

Annabel Dover, *Untitled [Stocking]*, 2012, cyanotype.

The grandmother went on to marry again, to a horrible bully. But she continued to pine for her missing husband. This feisty grandmother, full of longing for her lost first husband, fetishized her loss by keeping her sexy stockings (one of which was made into Dover's cyanotype), along with a nice silk handkerchief and some red lipstick in a drawer that remained locked up and sealed until her death in the late 1980s.

But the locked-up drawer (with stockings, handkerchief and lipstick) was not her only feat of fetishism. Also discovered, after the grandmother's death, sewn into the lining of her fur coat, was a pair of silky pink knickers (meant for the lost husband), as well as his photograph. (With her pink knickers tucked into the lining of fur, Dover claims her grandmother as a walking Méret Oppenheim sculpture.) It was when Dover's mother was going through the grandmother's things that the little booty of panties and photo was found. While checking the pockets, she felt the photograph and the silky pink knickers through the satin lining. Sometimes you *feel* something *missing* that you did not know you were looking for. What lovesickness.

Dover's blue stocking floats in a sea of blue, like Ophelia in the river:

> Her clothes spread wide
> And, mermaid-like, awhile they bore her up.

The blue stocking floats and emphasizes the tragic, biographical detail that, like Shakespeare's heroine who 'fell in the weeping brook', Dover's grandmother also died in the water. The artist's grandmother had a heart attack in a cool bath and thus, Ophelia gives way to Dover's grandmother. Both women give way to the Pre-Raphaelite model, artist and poet Elizabeth Siddall. She famously posed for John Everett Millais's painting of Shakespeare's most romanticized heroine, his *Ophelia* (1851–2). Of note is the story of the model gone cold. Indeed, while Siddall was floating as

Ophelia in a makeshift river contrived for the studio (a bathtub), the warming lamps beneath went out. Siddall turned very chilly, but she kept her silence. As a result, Siddall became very ill and nearly caught her death. The mythologies of these Ophelias, Elizabeth Siddall and Dover's grandmother, chill the heart. They both seem to say, 'take me'. As the American poet Natasha Trethewey writes of Siddall's 'catching cold':

> In Millais's painting, Ophelia dies faceup,
> Eyes and mouth open as if caught in the gasp
> of her last word or breath, flowers and reeds
> growing out of the pond, floating on the surface
> around her. The young woman who posed
> lay in a bath for hours, shivering,
> catching cold, perhaps imagining fish
> tangling in her hair or nibbling a dark mole
> raised upon her white skin. Ophelia's final gaze
> aims skyward, her palms curling open
> as if she's just said, *Take me.*[9]

Millais's painted *Ophelia* speaks mythologies of lovesickness through the language of flowers, particularly those hued blue. See the garland (a noose) of bluish violets looping Siddall's neck. Find along the river bank the blue forget-me-nots. Contemplate, atop Siddall's golden dress, those blue pansies, 'that's for thoughts'.

To read Dover's blue stocking as floating like Ophelia is a metaphor, and is to ask '"What is it? What does it mean"– the real question [Barthes tells us] of critical and philosophical writing'.[10] To read Dover's blue stocking as her grandmother is metonymic, and is to 'ask another question: "What can follow what I say? What can be engendered by the episode I am telling?": this is [Barthes tells us] the question of the Novel'.[11] For Barthes, philosophy is metaphor; the novel is metonymy. Barthes, like

Annabel Dover, *Untitled [Washing a cyanotype]*, 2012, photograph.

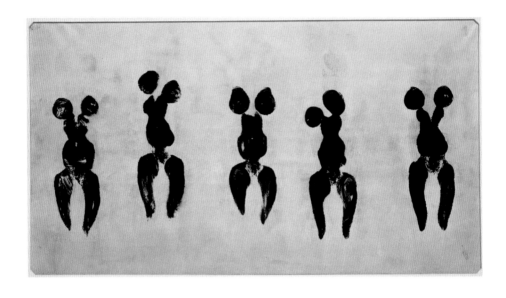

Yves Klein, *Anthropométrie de l'époque bleue,* 1960, pure pigment and synthetic resin
on paper mounted on canvas.

Proust, strives for both, and is 'metaphorico-metonymic', like
Dover's blue stocking.

The stocking is Ophelia (metaphor). The stocking is missing
(metonymy). It is the missing husband; it is displacement for the
grandmother's desire. She misses him. It is a divided subject. Like
this book. Like blue.

A FLOATING BLUE WORLD

Some of the first photographs were blue. The process of making
cyanotypes was a procedure discovered by Sir John Herschel
in 1842. He used it as a way to make *blueprints* in order to
save copies of notes and diagrams. But it was Anna Atkins who
brought the science to photography to make her limited series
books documenting stunning Yves Klein blue prints of botanical
specimens.

In 1853, Anna Atkins's poppy magically appeared in its own
pool of cyan blue.

The enchantment of Atkins's poppy developing in the wetness
of a pool of water springing slowly before her eyes is suggestive of
Proust's own miraculous Japanese paper flowers:

> And as in the game wherein the Japanese amuse themselves
> by filling a porcelain bowl with water and steeping in it little
> pieces of paper which until then are without character or
> form, but, the moment they become wet, stretch and twist
> and take on colour and distinctive shape, become flowers or
> . . . the water lilies on the Vivonne . . . the whole of Combray
> and its surroundings taking shape and solidity, sprang into
> being . . . from my cup of tea.[12]

The suggestive 'idleness' of Marcel's flowers and water lilies
coming into being, along with a host of countless other memories

of his boyhood's Combray, is marked by Barthes as 'a moment of writing'.[13] As Barthes writes, 'the Japanese paper flowers, tightly folded, that blossom and develop in water. That would be idleness: a moment of writing, a moment of the work.'[14]

In 1843, Anna Atkins made a book of sea algae. Floating, like a 'foam of daisies'[15] washed in from swelling folds of the ocean, the algae are fragments of short stories carried by the sea. The etymology of algae, which is Latin for seaweed, is obscure. Perhaps the word comes from *alliga*, which means 'binding and intertwining',[16] which sounds like letters on a page, only the blue ink is white and the white page is blue.

> The algae stories are wide-ranging:
> Some are feathery. *Dichloria viridis.*
> Some are strangely modern: *Laminaria fascia.*
> Some are like a flash of splintered lightning that has hit the
>   ground.
> Some are stick drawing.
> Some are forlorn Christmas trees without enough branches.
> Some are sewing threads.
> Some are frazzled, worn, satin ribbons.
> Some, like *Halyseris polypodioides* are milky gouache, more
>   gouache than watercolour because of the opaqueness.
> Some are pressed nasturtium flowers. *Padina pavonica.*
> Some are seashell fragments. Again a *Padina pavonica.*
> Some are cauliflower.
> Some are metal shrapnel.
> Some are burst spring onions.
> Some are the curly long hair pulled from a woman's brush
>   after a full week of combing.
> Some are the roots of a bean grown in a glass with a paper
>   towel in my kitchen window when I was six years old.
> Some are foxtails rushes.
> Some are a whimsical French print on a blue 1940s silk dress.

Anna Atkins, *Dictyota dichotoma*, from *Photographs of British Algae: Cyanotype Impressions,* PART I, 1843, cyanotype.

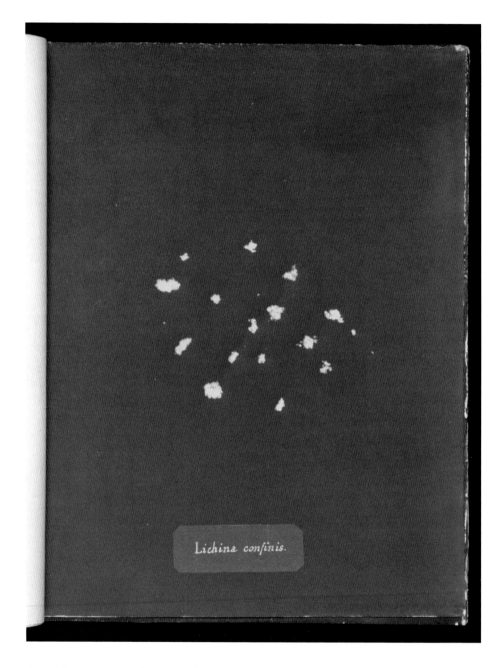

Anna Atkins, *Lichina confinis*, from *Photographs of British Algae: Cyanotype Impressions*, PART I, 1843, cyanotype.

Cystoseira granulata.

Anna Atkins, *Cystoseira granulata*, From *Photographs of British Algae: Cyanotype Impressions*, PART I, 1843, cyanotype.

The paper is cream.

Punctaria latifolia is a fleshly little woman standing in the
    sun in an almost sheer dress, waiting for the bus.

Something Rorschach about them.

Punctaria plantaginea is a Cycladic person.

One is my mother's nylon stocking scrunched up and alone,
    like many housewives felt in the 1960s.

Some are silk cocoons.

Some are a blown dandelion seed.

One is my grandmother's brooch.

Some are clumps of bits of earth.

Some are pieces of tiny coral.

Some are the transparent folds of a watery Delphos gown,
    made by Mariano Fortuny y Madrazo. *Laminaria
    bulbosa.*

Atkins's *Sea Algae* are particularly *thalasso-graphic* (sea-writing). Taking her specimens directly out of the ocean, her 'ocean flowers'[17] return to us in pools of blue and are *involuntarily* suspended outside of time in a floating world, like 'Japanese paper flowers, tightly folded, that blossom and develop in water . . . a moment of writing, a moment of the work'.[18]

11
Blue Lessons: *A Patch of Blue, a Blue Cardigan Buttoned and a Robin's Egg*

SALLY HOBART ALEXANDER's book for young people, entitled *Do You Remember the Color blue?*, describes what is is like to be a sighted person who has lost her vision. For Alexander, blue is the only colour that she seems to remember vividly: 'Because I could see for twenty-six years, I can remember the color blue. Say the word, and I picture robins' eggs, bluebirds, forget-me-nots, and cornflowers'.[1]

In France, the blue cornflower is the bloom for their Remembrance Day. In France, a cornflower (*bleuet* in French) is a blue poppy for remembering *blue*.[2]

Here is my blue cornflower memory: I was about ten years old, it was a day when I was ill and stayed home from school; but I was not too sick to enjoy myself. In a wash of afternoon light, while changing channels on the black-and-white television, I happened upon *A Patch of Blue* (1965), the heart-wrenching melodrama starring Sidney Poitier, directed by Guy Green, produced during the Civil Rights Movement. Selina (played by Elizabeth Hartman) is helpless, white, blind and adolescent, and has a terrible mother who caused her blindness during a drunken scuffle. The only colour memory that Selina has from her world before blindness is a 'patch of blue'. Blind Selina, with this bit of blue sky or blue ocean or blue cardigan or blue cup or blue nothing at all, falls in love with Gordon, who is a gorgeous 'man of colour' played by Poitier. Gordon gives Selina the lessons that her mother never taught her: how to use a telephone, how to cross a street. Gordon is paternally nurturing, feeding her everyday life. For Selina, who is inexperienced in all forms of being, this is surprisingly delicious.

For example, when Gordon gives her pineapple juice for the first time, she asks with astonishment, 'Wow, what is this delicious drink?' Gordon watches over Selina and allows her to learn; to *listen* for the sound of cars, the sound of the dime dropping into the pay phone before hearing the dial tone, and so on. Gordon does not tell Selina that he is black; she hears it from her mother and she learns it. Not only is Gordon a caring teacher, but he is handsome and sexy too. Selina can feel this. (Green could have made the film in colour, but he was emphatic that it be in black and white.) Nevertheless, my memory of that film is hued blue.

I am not a synaesthete, with memories of 'being born on a blue day'.[3] 'Wednesday' for me is not 'indigo blue'.[4] 'Cat' is not a 'blue word'[5]. Even as a child, I never heard a 'frog who croaked blue'.[6] But my memory of that day and the film that I watched is blue. On that day, *A Patch of Blue* took up residence inside me, as fragile and as strong as a robin's egg. Although I could only sense, and could not yet understand the film's sexual and racial awakenings, its colour lessons enabled me to hear my future mistakes: sexual, racial, prejudiced.

Laurie Colwin's 'Mr Parker' (1973) is a short story of an adolescent girl's lesson in sexuality, which also turns on blue, with a fragility and strength comparable to *A Patch of Blue*.[7] In both the film and the short story, the narrative is stingy with references to the colour blue; the ungenerosity is particularly powerful. *A Patch of Blue* and 'Mr Parker' both bestow blue with a strong presence, like an oratorio given by a single gentian on a grey rock.

In the short story, 'Jane' takes piano lessons from the middle-aged Mr Parker at his house. He 'had once been blond, but was greying into the colour of straw'[8]. Mr Parker goes into 'the City' to work on Wall Street; he studied at Juilliard. Hence, '[h]is playing was terrifically precise'.[9] Both Mr and Mrs Parker are autumnal: 'faded out of some bright time they once had lived in'.[10] Through slight emphases, like Baroque music and the aesthetics of their home, there is something vaguely sexual, at times bohemian, about the childless Parkers. The Parkers are interesting and are different from the middle-class families that I knew, or, it seems, from those that Jane and her family knew.

The story begins with Mrs Parker's sudden and tragic death. The parting of Mrs Parker makes the house, suddenly, inappropriate, according to Jane's mother, for piano lessons. ('The Brain – is wider than the Sky',[11] writes Emily Dickinson.) The situation is difficult to judge. For the story is a piano lesson, like one Mr Parker might give. 'Basically', Jane tells us, 'he wanted me to hear my mistakes'.[12]

Here are the blues. Mr Parker 'always wore a blue cardigan, buttoned'[13] on his piano-teaching days. And, at the close of the first lesson that Jane takes in Mr Parker's house (after the death of Mrs Parker), we received this scintillation: 'At the end . . . he gave me a robin's egg he had found. The light was flickering through the bunch of roses in the window as I left'.[14] These two blues markedly disrupt the general autumnal colours of the story, including not only Mr Parker's hair, but also Mrs Parker's, which was once red, but has turned the colour of 'old leaves',[15] the 'dried weeds in ornamental jars',[16] the 'chocolate brown' exterior of the old house, which 'faded to the colour of weak tea',[17] and so on. It is within this thirsty, earthy palette that we hear the blue times two. Once home, 'Jane wrapped the robin's egg in a sweat sock'.[18]

Just as we might ask why are the eggs of the American robin *Turdus migratorius* blue, we ask of Colwin's meticulously constructed story, why a *blue* cardigan buttoned and a robin's egg? Although we know that the blue of robin's eggs comes from a higher concentration of biliverdin, the scientific explanation behind *why* the robin's egg is blue 'has long defied explanation',[19] just as the blues of 'Mr Parker' are not clear. Recently, it has been discovered by Robert Montgomerie (an expert on sexual selection and parental care in birds) that male American robins invest more heavily in those nests with brighter blue eggs.[20] The more dazzling the blue of the eggs, the more attention the males give to their young. Males feed baby robins from nests containing the brightest blues twice as much. It seems that the higher the level of biliverdin in the eggs, the healthier the mother robin who laid them.

The blues of the robin's eggs are equally about sexuality and nurturance. The same is true for the blues of 'Mr Parker'. Yet, because 'Mr Parker' is a story about people, specifically a widower and an adolescent girl, and is not a scientific study about birds, these blues (sexual and nurturing) are paradoxical. The sweater had to be invested with blue. The egg had to be a robin's.

12
TO BLUE: *Helen Chadwick's Oval Court*

I live by the ocean
and during the night
I dive into it
down to the bottom
underneath all currents
and drop my anchor

this is where I'm staying
this is my home.

Björk Guðmundsdóttir[1]

EVERYTHING IS BLUE

In the mid-1980s, the British artist Helen Chadwick repeatedly placed her naked body on the glass of the photocopier, filled with blue ink and took images of her body, along with a cornucopia of surreal goods and chattels. There are fruits and vegetables: split open grapefruits and tomatoes, peeled and sectioned tangerines, leeks, onions, turnips, olives, rocket, a pineapple and figs. There are piles of fish: a monkfish, sardines, a ray and eels. There are heaps of furry and feathery animals: rabbits, a goose and mice. There are insects: bees and maggots. There are feminine possessions: lace, a mirror, ribbons, bangles, fishnet stockings and pearls. There is meat: tripe and a huge cow's tongue. There are plants from the fields: dandelions, wheat and thistles. There are practical objects for capturing, killing and chopping: knives, fishhooks, sinuous rope and an axe. There are beautiful objects from the natural world: seashells and feathers. All of these things (tangerines, rabbits, eels, ropes, fishhook stockings, fishhooks and much more) are tangled up in blue. Chadwick called the piece, in which she carefully and circumferentially arranged her blue photocopies very flatly on a slightly raised ovoid floor (piecing the cut-out paper pieces together in azure pools with the precision of a surgeon, a seamstress, a film editor), *Oval Court*.

The action of Chadwick's light-writing is the work of the *scriptor*, not an Author with a capital 'A'. As Barthes explains in his famed 1967 'Death of the Author', 'the modern scriptor is born simultaneously with the text, is in no way equipped with a being preceding or exceeding the writing, is not the subject with the book as predicate; there is no other time than that of the enunciation and every text is eternally written *here and now*.'[2] In Chadwick's *Oval Court*, the distance between the one who photographs and the photograph itself is dissolved by the process of the photocopy machine which yields, but does not take, as if it were performing the intransitive form of the verb, *to photograph*. Likewise, the colour blue yields meaning, but paradoxically will also give way to opposite meanings, as if it were performing the intransitive form of the verb, *to blue*.[3]

An intransitive verb expresses an action that does not pass over to an object: it does not take a direct object. Examples would be *to die, to be born, to fall, to sleep, to walk, to swim, to fly, to photograph* and, even, *to blue*. In the case of the intransitive form of the verb *to write*, which is of special interest to Barthes, the distance between the one who writes (the *scriptor*) and language itself is dissolved in the 'middle voice'.

TO WRITE, TO PHOTOGRAPH, TO BLUE

In 1966 Roland Barthes delivered a lecture at Johns Hopkins University (which was later published in English) entitled 'To Write: An Intransitive Verb?'.[4] This short piece is key to my understanding of Anna Atkins's cyanotypes and especially to the

blue photocopies that make up Chadwick's *Oval Court*. Chadwick's
and Atkins's *blueprints* are photographic equivalents of Barthes'
'To Write: An Intransitive Verb?' Their work seems to bespeak
an essay that Barthes never wrote, but might have, entitled:
'To Photograph: An Intransitive Verb?' Or even, 'To Blue: An
Intransitive Verb?'

Barthes was long planning *to write* – to write literature
(a novel) – but never did. In 1980 he was tragically killed during
the academic year in which he had been teaching his seminar
course entitled 'The Preparation of the Novel'. On his way to
deliver what would have been his last lecture at the Collège de
France, he was hit outside the Collège by a laundry truck: he
lingered, but eventually the injuries would cause him *to die*.
Written, but never delivered, the title of the lecture was 'Proust
and photography'. Indeed, it remains an undelivered, *intransitive*,
gesture of to *write*.

TO WRITE WITH LIGHT IN THE KEY OF BLUE: *Helen Chadwick's Oval Court*

> *Out of the copier, no longer separate from things . . .*
> Helen Chadwick

As Chadwick remarks, in regard to one of the full-body self-
portraits that make up the blue pools of *Oval Court* in which her
neck is tied to her feet by a rope and a cornucopia of fruits and
vegetables are convulsing from her mouth, 'She is gagging with
pleasure . . . She's bursting out of the basket, and fruit is bursting
out of her'.[5] The image and Chadwick's comments are disorient-
ing. Who is 'she' and where is 'she'? Chadwick chose the colour
blue because it skews our sense of gravity and perspective. As she
comments:

Helen Chadwick, 'Fruit is bursting out of her', *The Oval Court Series*, 1984–6, photocopies and assorted media.

It was always blue, right from the beginning. I was drawn
to blue – the thing I most identified with – in the rococo,
was the sense of a transfixed reality that's constantly pulsat-
ing within itself. And that's achieved by rhythms and
asymmetrical, sinuous line [*sic*], and it seemed to me that
the colour where one cannot determine gravity or perspective
is blue – it's the only one because of its suggestion of sea
and air.[6]

Chadwick indulges in the paradoxes of blue, not only the 'sea
and air', but also its innocence and obscenity (note the schoolgirl
bobby socks coupled with orifices), death and life (the animals
look alive, but they are dead), and so on.

There are twelve ponds of these Chadwick girl-women
(in one pool she wears the girlish bobby socks, in all of the blue
lagoons she is uninhibited, like the good parts of youth). The
blue-girls share a state of ecstasy, sometimes involving knives and
blindfolds. Bawdy, often abject, always beautiful, they echo the
'twelve gates of Paradise',[7] but there is no St Peter floating about.
But like St Peter's in Rome, there are *Salomonic* columns (remin -
iscent of Bernini's *baldacchino* in St Peter's Basilica) carefully
drawn on paper affixed to the walls surrounding the pool. Atop
each pair of 'barley-sugar columns' (a name sometimes given
for the *Salomonic*) are photocopies of Chadwick's floating head,
scrunched and crying tears of blue vegetal life. And, like St Peter's
(and like a fairy tale), there is gold. Five large gold spheres, perfectly
round golden eggs that diminish in size, but stay large (the biggest
could hold a fully grown Chadwick). The gold balls (the Princess's
pea writ gigantic) sit atop her lily pads of erotic-gorgeous-disgusting
life. Chadwick is like Narcissus with his reflection (only with
heaps of traditional and unusual subjects for her *natures mortes*).
(There is plenty of death that has been placed on the glass.)
As Marina Warner so rightly notes, she 'invents the reflections
in a pool of love, like the pond in which Narcissus saw himself,

by using an actual glass, the reproductive reflector of the photo-copier'.[8]

Chadwick's 'experiments with simulacra'[9] are written with light. Her body, along with her harvest of animals and trimmings, floats (like light) in a pool of blue. But unlike the conventional negative-positive photograph, Chadwick's *Grimm* fairy-tale outputs have immediacy akin to the early cyanotypes of flowers, ferns, algae and other botanical specimens made by Atkins. Both are white images floating in blue pools. Atkins's strange shapes of algae (which look like ribbons or threads or strange little fruits or a seashell or feathers or cocoons or flower petals or string beans or popped popcorn) share, along with Chadwick's cornucopia of objects (strings of pearls or feathers or girlie ribbons or her own Boucher *rump*,[10] or her school of sardines) a sinuousness of the Rococo and the femininity of a highly detailed cameo image.

As a London artist, it is likely that Chadwick would have seen the exquisite blue-and-white intaglio shell cameos housed at the Victoria and Albert Museum. Intaglio comes from *intagliare*, meaning 'to cut in', and these tiny objects, often in an oval form, suggest Chadwick's own cut *Oval Court* writ large, as in the sixteenth-century cameo of the Jewish heroine *Jael* (Yael). The shell that was once housed underneath the blue sea is cut to tell a milky, even creamy, white story that is rich with violence and beauty.

Jael murdered Sisera in order to save Israel. In the Old Testament's 'Book of Judges', we hear how Sisera 'asked for water' but 'she gave him milk / She brought forth cream in a lordly dish' (Judges 5:25). And while he was in this sweetened state, the killing takes place: 'And she hammered Sisera, she smote through his head. She crushed and pierced his temple' (5:26). In the tiny oval carved from shell, creamy Jael appears to be stepping 'out of the blue', out of the 'O' that encloses her and her story, like the ornamental letter that begins a Once-upon-a-time fairy tale. Like Shakespeare's Cleopatra who opens her mouth to speak: 'The little O, the earth' (*Antony and Cleopatra*).

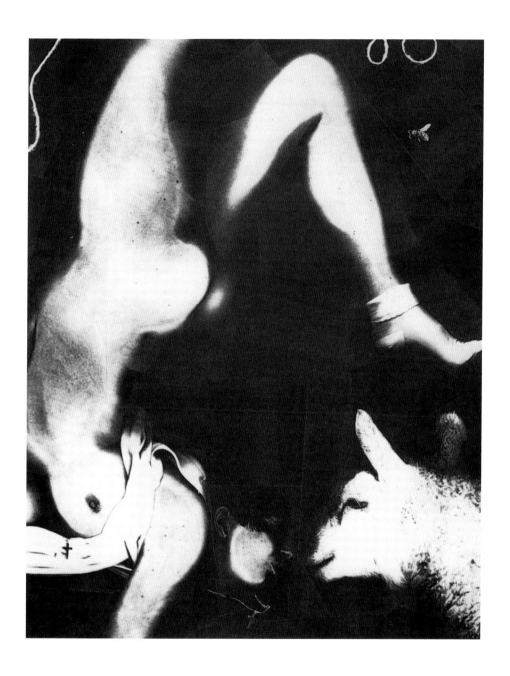

Helen Chadwick, 'Boucher rump', detail from *The Oval Court Series*, 1984–6.

Chadwick's body on the glass, quickly lit by the efficient mechanical squeegee of blinding light pulled beneath the glass by the photocopy machine, gives way to an emphasis on touch, which is akin with Atkins's botany work. Chadwick's breast had to touch the top of the glass, just as Atkins's algae had to touch the paper. Furthermore, each has an enchanting sense of the unexplained (even if we do know the science behind the cyano-type and the photocopy). *Touching* white magic in a blue pool. Chadwick's blue photocopies and Atkins' cyanotypes both share *immediacy*.

To write photography is always, in a sense, to leak into the fluidity of the utopian hold of the fairy tale. Photographs hold their referent (whether it is a goose, a breast, a starfish, a woman) as never changing. Photography's 'magic' casts the short-lived as forever and ever non-altered in an eternal emulsion of the frozen

Unknown, *Jael Cameo*, 16th century, France, carved shell.

time of Briar Rose's hundred-year-long sleep. Photographs make good the daguerreotype glass of Snow White's coffin.

But, of course, all photographs are not alike. I am concerned with the intransitive immediacy of the photocopied image and its unmechanical predecessor, the cyanotype. Other immediate forms of photography come to mind, like the Polaroid and the digital image. But these later forms (without requiring their subjects to touch the glass of the photocopier or the paper treated with cyanide salts) do not render the subject *intransitive*. The fairy-tale prints of *The Oval Court* mark the photo-grapher, the light-writer, and her subject as immediately contemporary (or nearly so) with the resulting image. Time is dissolved through the enchantment of the picture in which the image magically appears with uncanny propinquity as if one were stepping into Alice's looking glass turned photo-copy machine. Like an intransitive verb, the photocopy (like the cyanotype) does not *take* a direct object. Since the colour blue is particularly paradoxical, blue has no choice but to be intransitive.

In his important essay, 'Too-blue: Color-Patch for an Expanded Empiricism', Brian Massumi argues that we exaggerate the intensity of colour in memory. There, he highlights how the co-functioning of language, memory and affect tends to exaggerate colour, so much so that the memory of a friend's eyes might be recalled as 'too blue', even if they are not blue at all.[11] So, while memory might be 'too blue', *to blue* is to colour intransitively, openly, perhaps, utopically. *To blue* is *to write* with the light of the cyanotype, and in the case of Chadwick, the photo-copy machine.

I am reminded of a late eighteenth-early-twentieth-century watercolour brooch of a miniature eye. It is conveniently blue. It cries tears of diamonds. This watery eye is surrounded by pearls: a sign of whiteness and purity, not unlike milk, but certainly far more precious. Pearls are, of course, caused by an irritant in the oyster that produces a pearl. Here the irritated eye forms diamonds. But it is the point of the pin, as it sticks out from the back of the broach, which gives me a strange sort of Barthesian *punctum*, the word that he assigns to the part or detail of a photograph, with an alliteration of '*p*'s: *piqûre, petit trou, petite tache, petite coupure* ('prick', 'little hole', 'little spot', 'little cut')[12] which wounds or bruises.

Punctum is Latin for point. According to the *Oxford English Dictionary*, *punctum* is 'a very small division of time, an instant', 'a point used as a punctuation mark', and is part of the medical term, *punctum lacrimale*, meaning the 'tiny circular orifice from which tears emerge'. With Barthesian precision, brevity and style, *punctum* is at once a second of time, a non-alphabetical mark in writing and the tiny place from which tears come into view.

The cyanotypes of Atkins and the photocopies of Chadwick are too otherworldly to wound me with tears. They do something different. As has already been emphasized, they do not take. Instead, Atkins and Chadwick use the phrase '*to photograph*' intransitively, as an unfinished gesture, neither positive, nor negative; neither happy nor sad; neither alive nor dead; neither Virginal nor sexed; neither white nor black; neither expanding metaphor nor displacing metonymy, in a world where everything is blue.

Unknown, *Eye Miniature*, early 19th century, British, pearl surround, oil
on canvas miniature with diamond tears.

Bernard Perrot, Blue Glass Perfume Bottle, *c.* 1700, Orléans, glass and metal.

13
'A foggy lullaby'

THE ROMANTICS' LOVE of blue (as in Goethe's *Sorrows of Young Werther* of 1774 or Novalis's *Henry von Ofterdingen* of *circa* 1800*)* caused them to refer to fairy tales as 'blue tales'.[1] During those Goethe-blue-coat-yellow-vest and Novalis-blue-flower-days, a new perfume called '*Eau de Werther*' was invented.[2] Once *Eau de Werther* was released from its bottle, it could (like most scents) escape barriers. Apprehensible, yet invisible (that is, nothing), blue shares something with olfaction.

In about 1700, before Novalis and his blue flower, before Goethe and his blue-coat-yellow-vest, Bernard Perrot made a blue-glass scent bottle in the shape of a deeply moulded scallop shell. Its metal stopper is connected by a silvery chain. The back of the bottle is flat with a moulded design of a sun(flower). A paradox of blue: the bottle is both the shell from below, from the deep blue sea *and* as sun from above in the clear blue sky. The perfume bottle is a Janus head of sorts. It is not inconceivable, though perhaps only likely as a fantasy, that the blue scent bottle might have been filled up with *Eau de Werther* (the perfume created during the days of Werther madness).

> Blue, here is a shell for you
> Inside you'll hear a sigh
> A foggy lullaby.
>
> 'Blue', Joni Mitchell

Pietro Longhi, *Exhibition of a Rhinoceros at Venice*, c. 1751, oil on canvas.

14
WORDS FAIL

The wondrous rhinoceros Miss Clara was first captured in India
as an infant. She arrived in Holland in 1741 and was carted
across Europe for seventeen years. She is sadly pictured in Pietro
Longhi's painting, *Exhibition of a Rhinoceros at Venice* (c. 1751).
She has defecated. The small painting is of an overall light brown,
the colour of hay. But there is also the bright white of powdered
skin and carnival masks ('not lustrous but heavy, as disturbingly
dense as sugar'[1]) and the blacks of triangular hats. The tired greys
of Miss Clara's sartorial skin are in tune with the waistcoat of
the assistant who holds a whip. There is a splash of pink. I am
in the eighteenth century; I am reminded of the pink ribbon
that Charlotte wore when Werther first encountered her:

> Today is my birthday, and early in the morning a package
> arrived . . . When I opened it, the first thing I set eyes on was
> one of the pink ribbons Lotte was wearing when I met her,
> which I had often asked her for since then . . . I have been
> kissing that bow a thousand times over, and with every breath
> I take the memory of those few happy, irrecoverable days
> returns to me.[2]

A wrap of green. A bit of gold. A patch of yellow (or buff).
A pool of light blue bodice. I am now reminded of Werther's
blue frockcoat, which Werther had first worn when he first
danced with Charlotte. Eventually and famously it became so
threadbare that Werther had a 'new one made exactly like the
other'.[3] Werther's blue frockcoat and yellow vest are tailored
to repeat where words fail. As Roland Barthes comments in
A Lover's Discourse:

It is in this garment (blue coat and yellow vest) that Werther wants to be buried, and which he is wearing when he is found dying in his room. Each time he wears this garment (in which he will die), Werther disguises himself. As what? As an enchanted lover: he magically re-creates the episode of the enchantment, the moment when he was first transfixed by the Image. This blue garment imprisons him so effectively that the world around him vanishes: *nothing but the two of us . . .* This perverse outfit was worn across Europe by the novel's enthusiasts, and was known as a 'costume à la Werther'.[4]

Miss Clara is meant to steal the show but it is the woman in blue who steals it for me. She takes the cake. It is she that I long for. In the distance, she beckons me with her blue silence. (She is my Wertherian Charlotte. My Lotte. My Lottchen.) Her mask perversely insures that she cannot speak. She is as wordless as Miss Clara. She is even more mute than Miss Clara. While the other masked figures in the front row are wearing the *bauta*, this blue woman wears the *domino*: an oval black mask kept in place by a button held between the teeth, an arrangement which rendered its wearer temporarily speechless.[5] Her face becomes a single surreal eye and a huge open mouth, like a Francis Bacon silent scream.

The woman imprisoned in blue and by the *domino* echoes the soundless shrieks of Bacon's *Study after Velázquez's Portrait of Pope Innocent X* or his *Three Studies for Figures at the Base of a Crucifixion*.

Beyond the missing 'speech' of the woman in blue who wears the *domino*, something more is missing. Miss Clara is missing her horn. (It is in the hand of the assistant in the front row.) Words may fail, but you can hear the blue: it speaks a missing language.

Pietro Longhi, 'Woman in mask with bird', detail from *Exhibition of a Rhinoceros at Venice*, *c.* 1751, oil on canvas.

The colours of violets are variations on the hue of blue: purplish-blue, bluish-purple. In 1872, Edouard Manet painted *Bouquet of Violets* and gave it to the Impressionist painter Berthe Morisot. It is a tiny painting of the same bouquet that Morisot held in Manet's painting *The Balcony.* Violets are metonymically linked, at least through the painterly hands of Manet, to Morisot. Anne Higonnet describes Manet's small, lovely and intense gift of a painting of a bouquet of violets as follows: 'beside a partly folded note on which some words can be read and others not: "To Mlle Berthe, . . . Manet"? [. . .] An extraordinary thank-you note. A note in which words fail, disappear, become an image'.[6]

But the blues of the violets succeed in telling her what cannot, perhaps, be written. (Like Manet's special interest for this successful woman painter married to his brother.)

> *Roses are red*
> *Violets are blue*
> *And . . .*

A call out of the violet-blue.

Edouard Manet, *Bouquet of Violets*, 1872, oil on canvas.

Helen Sear, *Pond*, 2011, photograph.

15
A Blue Fawn's Eye

BLUE IS THE COLOUR of memory, of dreams. I return to Miró's 1925 *Photo*, on which, underneath a little island of thick blue paint, Miró has written in lovely black script '*Ceci est la couleur de mes rêves*' (This is the colour of my dreams). *Photo*, in French and English, is a snapshot. This is a snapshot of 'my dreams'. It is blue at its edges and in its depths. Blue is the colour of memory.

I close my eyes and I remember a really blue time from my childhood. I am remembering the blue eyes of a fawn. My family was vacationing in the summer in the Grand Teton National Park in Wyoming, where lakes and ponds and even the nearby thermal pools at Yellowstone National Park 'are like blue eyes staring at the blue sky'.[1] (I have seen such 'eyes' of the earth in California, North Carolina, New Zealand and England. Here is a frozen one from Wales, as photographed by Helen Sear in January 2011, about which she writes of moving 'one foot gingerly after the other, towards the centre of your eye'.[2]) I was with my mother when suddenly, 'out of the blue', a photographer, weighed down with equipment, appeared. He asked us if we wanted to see a fawn that had been left alone while its mother had gone to look for food. Mysteriously and uncharacteristically for my mother, we quickly agreed to follow this unknown man, who looked a little dangerous to me. And, as if in a fairy tale, we came upon one of most beautiful things that I have ever seen in my entire life: a fawn so young that its soft fur appeared moist. Its white spots looked magical and royal, inversions of the ermine trim of the fairy tale king's robe. Tiny blue forget-me-not flowers were flourishing around this beautiful thing curled up upon itself in perfect sleep, 'rocking to the rhythm of its heart and lungs'.[3] (But were the flowers really there, I wonder?) 'Don't touch', the photographer whispered to me.

The fawn's eyes were shut off from the world by a pair of
soft brown almond-shaped curtains. I could not see its eyes, but
I remember them as blue. My memory is cast in the blue of the
wide open skies of Wyoming, the delicate flowers and the fawn's
unseen eyes. My memory 'is blue at its edges and in its depths'.[4]
This fawn's eye from the taxidermist is, in my mind's eye, the ideal
Photo (in Miró's sense of the term) of that day that I remember
as so blue.

BLUE IS THE COLOUR OF MEMORY

Undoubtedly, I have exaggerated the blueness of my memory in
my blue-prone memory-bank. My memory of the sleeping fawn
is 'in some way too blue: excess'.[5] This fawn's eye, luminous blue-
grey, a strange little gift from a student given to me long ago
(which I kept on my desk when I lived under the famous blue
skies of North Carolina, which I carried with me across the sometimes blue Atlantic, and now stares back at me under the grey,
hardly ever blue, skies of England) has become a fetish for me.
I thought it was because it held onto the colour of a particular
memory from my childhood, that of the eyes of a fawn never seen.

But now, in it, I see the eyes of my mother, luminous blue-grey,
which have, because of illness and age, forgotten me, have, even,
forgotten herself. What remains is not she. She is now nearly
emptied of life. Her once sky-blue eyes are clouded. The fawn's eye
stares at me and sees nothing. I think of her. 'I do it as an exercise'.[6]

I hold my mother's weak, but strongly gnarled hand, long past
its bloom. Over-touched by sun, wind, soap, cold, age, it is spotted
and withered, but very soft. Her desperate, enlarged blue veins (like
stems of old roses) are just under the surface of withered petal-thin
skin. Inside my head is a picture of the girl she once was, a girl I
never knew, the girl-as-flower in Novalis's blue fairy tale (*Henry von
Ofterdingen*): 'Her face was like a lily inclined towards the rising

sun, and from her slender white neck, the blue veins clung round
her tender cheeks in gentle curves'.[7] My mother's veins are too-loud
echoes of her once thin girl-veins.

My mother is 'lodged in me like a knife, and yet I am beginning to forget her. Already the image of her that I hold in my
head is fraying like bits of pigments, flakes of Memory's gold
leaf, are chipping off'.[8] My memory is beginning to flake like
the decorative gold band painted on the Virgin's blue headdress
on Pedro de Mena's polychromed *The Virgin of Sorrows* (*Mater
Dolorosa*, *c.* 1673).[9] Likewise, my mother's (glass) tears are also
long gone. My mother no longer cries. I am not sure she can.
But one can sense the stains of where my mother's real tears once
were, just as one can see the marks of where the glass tears once
were on Mena's *The Virgin of Sorrows*. Blue is eye of the fawn,
the iris of my mother.

That fawn's eye that I never saw but remembered blue made a
home for itself inside me, like Joseph Cornell's ultramarine marble

Found Object (Fawn's Eye).

that he has fit snug into the centre of the body of a book entitled *Rosalba.* My mother is 'swallowed and preserved'.[10] She is an untranslated and untranslatable trauma.

How does one mourn someone still alive, yet who is not of this world? How does one impossibly mourn, in other words, how does one mourn without end, without forgetting? One hues it blue.

Through age and time, my mother has become a little girl and I have become old. Roles are inversed. But I want to inverse it again. I eat as child. I remedy my oral (and emotional) vacancy by eating my mother. I eat blue. I eat my mother alive, in order to bury her within myself. 'Swallowed and preserved. Inexpressible mourning erects a tomb inside'[11] me, a concept I have come to understand through the *mourning mouth-work* of psychoanalysts Nicolas Abraham and Mária Török.

Psychoanalysis meets the fairy tale: I become the Witch wanting to eat Hansel, the Wolf wanting to eat Little Red Riding Hood, the Wicked Queen wanting to eat Snow White's lungs and liver. I invert the famed line, 'My father, he ate me' (from Grimms's 'Juniper Tree'), into, 'My mother, I ate her'.

Through the work of Karl Abraham, I understand that I have an 'oral fixation'.[12] I understand, like Abraham's patient, that 'loving somebody' is 'exactly the same as the idea of eating something good'.[13] I consume 'like a descendent of the oral stage';[14] I swallow my mother, 'skin, hair, clothes and all'.[15] I swallow her, not as she is now, but as she once was. My mother is swallowed inside me, just as I was inside her. To eat my blue mother is to eat like a child, to (ch)eat death.

Blue blossoms and blooms into blues within blues. I am under my mother as sky. I am bowered by the Virgin's cloak in Zurbarán's *Virgin of Mercy.* I am under a blue sky, near a blue lake, staring at the closed blue eyes of a fawn, circled with blue forget-me-nots.

Pedro de Mena, *The Virgin of Sorrows*, *c.* 1673, painted wood, ivory, glass and human hair (detail).

16

'Blue Albertine' and 'Blue Ariane' (*Marcel Proust and Chantal Akerman*)

Nietzsche's prophecy: 'A labyrinthine man never seeks the truth but only his Ariadne'.

Roland Barthes, *Camera Lucida*

ALBERTINE IS AS DUPLICITOUS AS THE COLOUR BLUE

Proust's aquamarine-eyed 'Albertine', who is the novelist's most noted character in his multi-volumed *In Search of Lost Time*, is as duplicitous, is as promiscuous, as the colour blue. In tome III, Albertine is *La Prisonnière* or *The Captive*; in tome IV, she is *Albertine disparue* or *The Fugitive*. These telling titles of 'captive' and 'fugitive' are in tune with Albertine's paradoxical nature. Just as critics argue over whether to name the protagonist of the *Search* as the Narrator or 'Marcel', 'Marcel' never knows if Albertine is telling the truth or telling a lie. Likewise, Albertine is lovable *and* unlovable. Albertine is ignorant *and* smart. Albertine is beautiful *and* unattractive (from the front she is gorgeous, from the side, she is hooked-nosed like a Leonardo caricature). Albertine lives with Marcel and she comes to his bed, yet she is a lesbian. Furthermore, one can never tell if Albertine is a character of memory or forgetfulness. She is always changing, just as water can be ice and steam. All one can say is that she is impossible to hold onto, like water itself. Yet, Proust does not *really* want to know if Albertine is a lesbian, if she speaks the truth, where she has been, et cetera. Why doesn't he? Because *to know* enables mourning and he does not want to be cured of the illness of mourning. 'Is there any need to know a fact?',[1] ponders the Narrator, some 100 pages into the start of *The Captive,* the long and impossible mourning-story of Albertine.

Beautiful blue is everywhere in the two Albertine books. The colour unfolds and refolds, like the ocean waves that embody Albertine; like the madeleine cake, 'molded in the fluted valve of a scallop shell'[2] and whose folds hold the secrets of the novel. The madeleine, 'so richly sensual under its severe, religious folds',[3] is a metonymy to Albertine. As an 'underwater' memory, Albertine is a floating and sinking vestige of the 'shell', the 'aquatic' mould to which the madeleine refers in Proust's liquid *Search*.[4] Mutually reflective in hue and meaning, Albertine and blue are inseparable. Even her black hair has the blue of violets. As Proust writes of Albertine, 'what could be more beautiful than that clustering coronet of black violets?'[5] Albertine is Marcel's blue valentine.

ALBERTINE IS THE SEA

Albertine is one with the sea. 'All round her hissed the blue and polished sea',[6] writes Proust of Albertine. Within Albertine shines the 'blue-green undulations of the sea'.[7] In the words of Proust:

> The very emptiness of her life gave Albertine a sort of eagerness to comply with the only requests that I made of her. Behind this girl, as behind the purple light that used to filter beneath the curtains of my room at Balbec, while outside the concert blared, were shining the blue-green undulations of the sea'.[8]

Or, recall, how Proust writes of Albertine's blue sea-side eyes:

> Her blue, almond-shaped eyes, grown longer, had not kept their form; they were indeed of the same colour, but seemed to have passed into a liquid state. So much so that, when she shut them it was as though a pair of curtains had been drawn to shut out a view of the sea.[9]

ALBERTINE IS LOST LIGHT, SEALED TIGHT, AND SILENT

You cannot see her. Albertine is held captive in Marcel's apartment as shell. But like scent, she can slip through barriers. This is why, even when she is right before the eyes of Marcel, before her readers, she cannot be found. (This 'Ariadne' provides no string.) She is too blue. She is the blue sky. An atom of blue within blue. The colour blue, as we know from Rebecca Solnit, is made up of the 'light that got lost', which paradoxically 'gives us the beauty of the world, so much of what is in the color blue'.[10] Albertine, she, too, is that blue beauty, that light that got lost.

You cannot touch her. In the words of Proust:

> I could, if I chose . . . hold her head in my hands, I could caress her, run my hands slowly over her, but just as I had been handling a stone which encloses the salt of immemorial oceans or the light of a star, I felt that I was touching no more than a sealed envelope of a person who inwardly reaches to infinity . . . the marvellous captive.[11]

You cannot hear her. Hardly a word out of the blue from Albertine. Despite the fact Albertine's name is mentioned 2,360 times, more than any other character in the novel. Albertine is as silent as a clear blue sky. (She is as silent as Pietro Longhi's woman wearing pale blue, clenching the button of the *domino* between her teeth while staring at Miss Clara.[12]) We hear the name of Swann 1,643 times. We hear the name of Mama 210 times. We hear the name of Mother 1,407 times.[13] That is why Jacqueline Rose gave her a voice in her novel entitled *Albertine*. But to give her voice is to take away her loud silent presence.

ALBERTINE IS A FORTUNY GOWN

Albertine covets the expensive gowns made by the Venetian designer Mariano Fortuny, whose dresses were inspired by Carpaccio and Titian. The great Spanish designer, who made his home and reputation in the watery city of Venice, takes the shimmering water that surrounds him as his primary metaphor. Fortuny was part of the 'wave of Orientalism that swept through the world of fashion' in the years before the First World War.[14] 'Working like an artisan and researching like an alchemist',[15] Fortuny dyed his own fabrics for his mythic gowns. Fortuny used pigment over pigment, like Proust used words over words (the latter revising and extending his notebooks with his famed *paperoles*, by folding pages into accordion pleats that could fold out into lengths of over four feet). The fabric for Fortuny's gowns were painstakingly layered (rewritten) to perfection with richly coloured natural dyes and often with the addition of a patina of gold or sliver. The shimmering folds of his gowns, and, in particular, the famous pleats of his Delphos gown, reflected the city of water, and all that was Venice. In the words of Proust:

> The Fortuny gown which Albertine was wearing that evening seemed to me the tempting phantom of that invisible Venice, like the Venetian palaces hidden like sultan's wives behind a screen of perforated stone, like the binding of the Ambrosian Library, like the columns from which oriental birds that symbolised alternatively life and death were repeated in the shimmering fabric of an intense blue, which as my eyes drew nearer, turned into a malleable gold by those same transmutations, which before an advancing gondola change into gleaming metal the azure of the Grand Canal. And the sleeves were lined with a cherry pink, which is so peculiarly Venetian that it is called Tiepolo pink.[16]

Fortuny worked to frame the face, often hiding the feet. Importantly, Fortuny gowns were never meant to be worn outside as street dress or even ball gowns. They were dressing gowns, 'experimental indoor robes',[17] explicitly made for an interior world. Fortuny expected women to wear the dresses, inside, without shoes. In a photograph (1920) of Lilian Gish she wears a Fortuny gown that adheres to the shapely curves of this silent film star, like oil on water: her drapery shines, ripples and pleats with cling. She looks nude, but not naked. Her feet are swaddled in wetness. She has just emerged from a pool, a lagoon. Wendy Ligon Smith has described the mermaid-like women wearing their fish-scale-like folds of Fortuny Delphos gowns as having 'puddles around their feet'.[18] To wear a Delphos gown is to be dressed and undressed at once, just as Albertine is captive *and* fugitive. Albertine is blue inside and out, like a Delphos gown in blue. Exquisite is Albertine with her 'Fortuny gown in blue and gold . . . of a blue and virginal water'.[19] In her watery folds (like Proust's madeleine, like Fortuny's Delphos gown) Albertine holds her own *madeleinesque* secrets.

ARIANE IS BLUER THAN ALBERTINE

Chantal Akerman's 2000 film entitled *The Captive*, like tome III of Proust's *In Search of Lost Time*, is rich with the azures, cobalts and ceruleans of the bluest parts of Proust's 4,300-page novel. But Chantal Akerman's modernized, feminized, supra-lesbian-ized reworking of Proust's *The Captive* renames the famed Albertine as 'Ariane'. 'Ariane' is French for 'Ariadne'. Ariadne, of course, is the famed mythological figure who provides Theseus with the string that enables him to find his way out of the maze. Akerman's renaming of Proust's Albertine as 'Ariane' is ironic for, in Akerman's film, this Ariane reveals 'nothing', save for her paradoxical blueness. (Akerman also renames the

Titian, *Bacchus and Ariadne, c.* 1520–23, oil on canvas.

Narrator or 'Marcel' of Proust's *The Captive,* as 'Simon'. But his
name is without the connected 'mythology'.)

The ultramarine in Titian's 1523 painting of *Bacchus and
Ariadne* (which the artist began in Venice and finished in Ferrara),
housed in London's National Gallery, 'is of the most intense colour
and high purity of any so far met with', claims Joyce Plesters. [20]
(Plesters spent the whole of her working life, from 1949 to her
retirement in 1987, in the Scientific Department of the National
Gallery.) In regard to *Bacchus and Ariadne,* she notes that Titian,
as a Venice painter with wealthy clients, 'would have had first pick
of all of the materials'. [21] She notes that '*Natural (lapis lazuli) ultramarine...* is the predominant blue pigment – one might almost
say the predominant pigment – in the picture ... in the sky ...
the lights and middle tones of blue drapery, the iris and the
columbine flowers... it is found in Ariadne's blue cloak and
the drapery of the Bacchante with the cymbals'. [22] It is a rich
and intense painting, metaphorically and materially. Indeed,
'the cheaper blue pigments, indigo and smalt, are conspicuous
by their absence'. [23]

Albeit through film, Akerman takes Proust's Albertine on a
similar blue pilgrimage, swallowing her deep into the sea. [24] We
sense this from the very start of the film, in which we meet Ariane
in a Super 8 home movie. Ariane is at the seaside with her band
of lesbian friends. Ariane and her blue eyes and the blue beach
ball that she tosses about are tangled up in the blue of the sea.

Akerman's *The Captive* begins and ends with the sea, begins
and ends with blue, the light that got lost. Like Hans Christian
Andersen's 'Little Mermaid', Ariane throws herself into the
sea. We do not know if Ariane felt her body dissolve into foam.
For, really, we know nothing of Ariane (and for that matter,
of Albertine).

IN ONE OF the most beautiful blue scenes in Akerman's *The Captive*, which showers onto the screen steely grey-blues, fish-scale blues and blue-blacks, we find Simon soaking in the bathtub. On the other side of the clear-pebbled glass that serves as a wall between the two bathtubs is Ariane, washing in a bathtub and later standing to use a hand-held shower head. She is talking and singing. Simon confesses that, yesterday, when she was asleep next to him and her peignoir fell open, he looked at her vagina. He parted her legs ever so slightly. He wanted to know. He wanted to see. Did she mind?, he asks. 'No', she replies, 'do as you like'. He touches her through the glass, as if she were in a glass aquarium. She is partitioned from him. They are both cast in blue. They are wet. It is hard to say who is captive of who, who is fugitive. The view is neither intimate nor distanced. It is neither inside nor outside. It is the neither-nor space of being in love, as described by Barthes in *A Lover's Discourse*: 'The world plays at living behind a glass partition; the world is an aquarium; I see every-thing close up and yet cut off, made of some other substance'.[25] There's a blue frostiness to the scene, despite the steam, not unlike the ices that Albertine loves, 'raspberry obelisks' with the 'glory of Coolness', which she desires to 'melt deep down' in her 'throat'.[26]

Simon's aquarium keeps his little Ariane-Mermaid, but the glass between them cannot be broken, for it is as liquid as she is, as liquid as blue. He will never capture her.

He will never know her.

And nowhere is this blue girl (whether she be Albertine or Ariane) more *designified* than when she is asleep. And it is when she is asleep, or feigning sleep, that he embarks upon her, fully clothed, so as to be 'gently rocked'[27] by her steady breathing. Marcel is not interested in penetration.

Akerman's film has two long scenes of this non-coital rowing and wingbeating sleep. We are about to witness one of these 'rowing' sex scenes. Ariane is asleep (or awake?) in her bower bed of blue. Simon has come to her. While we watch this slow scene, I will read to you a passage from Proust in which he describes Marcel's non-penetrating sleep-sex with Albertine. Listen to how the words are rich with metaphors of the blue sea and the blue sky:

> Sometimes [her sleep] afforded me a pleasure that was less pure. . . . I . . . allowed my leg to dangle against hers, like an oar which one trails in the water, imparting to it now and again a gentle oscillation, like the intermittent wing-beat of a bird asleep in the air. . . . The sound of her breathing, which had grown louder, might have given the illusion of the panting of sexual pleasure, and when mine was at its climax, I could kiss her without having interrupted her sleep. I felt at such moments that I had possessed her more completely, like an unconscious and unresisting object of dumb nature. I was not troubled by the words that she murmured [in the film she cries out for her female lover] . . . [for] it was upon *my* hand, upon *my* cheek. . . . I savoured her sleep with a disinterested soothing love, just as I would remain for hours listening to the unfurling of the waves.[28]

In Proust's novel, Albertine dies in a horse-riding accident. In Akerman's film, Ariane appears to have drowned. She cannot be found in the blue ocean. Again, there is no string to follow. Yet, Ariane has *not vanished*, for there was nothing there to lose. She was always already lost. Impossible to remember, yet impossible to forget: she is impossible to mourn. Impossible as Novalis's famed blue flower. As Colette writes on the subject of blue flowers, '[a]part from the monkshood aconite, scilla, lupin, love-in-the-mist, germander speedwell, lobelia, and that con-volvulus which outvies every other blue, the Creator of all things showed a certain close-fistedness when distributing our share of blue flowers.[29] A flower company can kidnap the gene from a petunia that is responsible for the blue in not only petunias, but also irises, violets and morning glories to try to make blue roses, but such a flower is really more imagination than reality.[30] Proust *kidnapped* Albertine and made a blue rose that was more imagination than reality.

Proust, like the male Satin Bowerbird, made use of seemingly everything that passed his way, especially if it was blue, in order to construct an Albertine bower, a bachelor pad. Not a nest. Not a home.

But the capture is fleeting, because as soon as the Satin Bowerbird has his girl-bird, has, in a sense, 'clipped her wings',[31] he is ready to be rid of her and she leaves for a life alone, and must build her own nest. As 'Marcel' writes of Albertine at the end of *The Captive*, 'because the sea breeze no longer puffed out her skirts . . . because I had clipped her wings . . . she had ceased to be a winged Victory and become a burdensome slave of whom I would have liked to rid myself'.[32] Marcel is a real Emily Dickinson who won't come out.

It might be easier
To fail –with Land in Sight –
Than gain – My Blue Peninsula –
To perish – of Delight –
                    Emily Dickinson, *c.* 1862

In response, Akerman is 'out', and turns Proust's novel inside out. Proust's feminine excess becomes handsome austerity. Albertine becomes Ariane. Ariane-as-Albertine returns to the blue and joins her band of girls tossing a blue ball. She perishes of delight. Akerman's Ariane is even bluer than Proust's Albertine.

Ariane is 'ultramarine', in that she is 'beyond the sea'. With the understanding that 'ultra' means on the far side or beyond, we see why the blue pigment manufactured from lapis lazuli

BLUE Book

(Impossible?)

Blue Roses

from

Blue Rose hat

Magazine entitled

Intelligent Life Intelligence

→

AUTUMN 2008

Blue Roses, from the author's notebook, 2011.

was first described in Europe as *ultramarine*. Indeed, it had to be imported from the Middle East, 'beyond the sea'.[33] We experience Albertine as blue, but Ariane as ultramarine.

17

A Blue Lollipop
(*Krzysztof Kieślowski*)

IN KRZYSZTOF KIEŚLOWSKI'S 1993 film *Bleu*, Julie makes corrections, blue notes in blue pen, upon the black notes of her late husband's musical score. The blue ink stains her fingers like blood. Julie, like all seven of the characters in Kieślowski's trilogy of three films – *Blue – Red – White*, turns out to be the only survivor of a ferry accident. They did not drown in the blue sea– but they are all dark and all wear that Pola-blue, 'bruised underwater look'.[1] ('God made the sea to look through the window', Gabriel García Márquez.[2])

Driving, driving, driving. Living, living, living. A young daughter, who lives in a blue room at home, is dreamy and is holding the silver and blue wrapper of a lollipop recently devoured out of the window. The wrapper flashes as a greeting, but we sense it as a goodbye to the world. There is something in the air. It catches small bits of light and flashes. It is luminescent, despite this day's grey-blue sky. Its crackling sound and its silver-blue colour are satisfying. As Julia Kristeva notes, 'Colour is bodily; it is erotic. It comes from the body, like voice'.[3]

Anna lets go of the wrapper. Anna and her father will soon be dead. A car accident. We hear the sound of the crash, before we see anything. The bad luck of life. The mother will survive. The bad luck of life. The mother cannot survive because she cannot mourn.

Not long after this tragedy, the mother returns to the home where she had once lived happily with her husband and daughter. It is night. Almost everything has been cleared out of the house. She empties her handbag on the bare mattress and finds, by chance, another one of those blue lollipops. She had been saving it for her daughter, but that daughter is dead. So she eats it herself.

But unlike Proust's, homey, nostalgic madeleine, which gives way to all of his boyhood memories, from which he takes only a few nibbles, crumbs really, softly soaked in lime blossom tisane, Julie eats and crunches the blue lollipop with a ferocious tenderness; she is ravenous and angry.

For children, flavours are often inseparable from the artificial colours they love. At the snow-cone stand, you can ask a child what flavour they want and they will reply 'red' or 'blue'. Blue is a favourite flavour of youth. The list of *natural* blue foods is brief, and includes most obviously blueberries, but also the blue potato, plums (but are they not more black and purple than blue?), blue corn, the blue-milk oozing *Lactarius indigo* mushroom and blue cheese, which is mould and generally only liked by adults.

'Tomorrow they might have blueberry muffins for breakfast, so buy yourself a blue velvet cape today', writes Francesca Woodman (1958–1981), in her journal at age 17. A photographer, Woodman is most famous for her blurry soft-focus, surreal photographs of herself and her girlfriends (mostly nude or in advanced stages of undress). But Woodman also made cyan photographs, blueprint photographs (diazotypes), like her gorgeous, life-size *Caryatid* (1980). Here, her body is fully draped in folds, it is part marble carving, part Fortuny, part Proustian *paperole*. The tone is violet-blue. Her eyes and her mouth are shielded by her own lovely youthful arms. 'I think about food a deal of the time', continues the late-adolescent Woodman in her journal.

> Pastries are my favorite art form and I make beautiful . . .
> blackberry slump. Nothing more relaxing than settling down
> with a good cookbook and the words! I'm still thinking about
> some sweet narrow plums I ate in Italy last summer known
> as 'Nun's thighs'.[4]

In her 1980 diazotype, *Girl with Weed*, we are privy to succulent thighs like blue plums.

'When we are children', Proust tells us, 'we try to find the moon and the stars in books'. We are enraptured when the moon is a glistening luminary, 'and are disappointed by it . . . [when] it is compared to a cheese . . . cheese seems vulgar to us and the moon appears divine'.[5]

Blue snow cones, blue cotton candy (also called 'papa's beard' or 'candy floss'), blue ice cream (often in bubblegum flavour) or blue JELL-O, are all made for the taste of the child only.

Kieślowski's Julie eats childhood; a flavour walled off in blue, like her daughter's now empty azure bedroom. She swallows her daughter Anna. Julie's eating of the blue lollipop is an eating of Anna in order to bury her within herself, just as I imagined the eating of my own mother, when reflecting on childhood memories.[6]

When the mother weans her infant, language grows out of the child's empty mouth. Hence, 'the transition from a mouth filled with the breast to a mouth filled with words occurs by virtue of the intervening experiences of the empty mouth'.[7] You learn to talk when your mouth is no longer full. Emptiness gives way to desire and language.

But what happens when the child no longer is a mouth for the mother to feed, when the child no longer presents her with the empty mouth for her to coax words out of, to turn her now gone milk into speech? Julie remedies this oral vacancy left by

Francesca Woodman, *Girl with Weed*, New York, 1980, diazotype.

Anna by eating her child. Julie eats the child as food, swallows her whole in order to entomb her.

Before eating the blue lollipop that looks like a blue tongue, like the tongue of the dead, Julie sleeps with her late husband's friend. In an echo of Karl Abraham's discussion of the oral stage, Julie's sexuality is coupled with her cannibalistic impulses.[8]

Just as I imagined swallowing my mother blue, so as to remedy the vacancy in my heart, Julie opens her own mouth to her daughter's closed mouth. Julie swallows Anna, 'skin, hair, clothes and all.'[9] Just as I opened my mouth to the closed mouth of my mother-as-child, that is, my mother (as my little girl), who has forgotten me, who has forgotten how to eat, who has forgotten how to talk.

Julie claims she does not want to hold onto anything. But after swallowing Anna's lollipop, after making this blue tomb for her daughter inside herself, she decides to take with her the curious mobile composed of blue glass crystals that once hung below the light of her daughter's blue bedroom. For a while, she keeps it entombed in a cardboard box. She eventually lets it out, lets it shine in her new apartment.

The flautist on the street says to Julie, 'You gotta hold onto something'. What better way is there than to eat that something, that object, that person? Julie turns her mouth, emptied by the death of her child, into something productive: there is, eventually, the completion of the unfinished musical score and, even, the nurturance of her late husband's child, conceived with his mistress. Here, the image of the pregnant mistress is a repeat of Julie (metaphorically) swollen with the swallowing of Anna, or, even, the cat that Julie borrowed so that it would eat the nest of baby mice in her apartment. The womb and tomb nest within one another.

Anna's blue mobile is the same colour and texture as Roger Hiorns's 2008 installation of copper sulphate crystals writ large, entitled *Seizure*. For this remarkable project, Hiorns took a tiny, condemned, depressing, too small, worn out council flat near the

Elephant and Castle in south London and turned its interior into a sparkling blue jewel. A blue grotto. The effect of walking into the semi-darkness of the small habitat is to be struck again by Julia Kristeva's '*le bleu de Padoue*' (Padua's blue), only in London in the twenty-first century. Hiorns's is a tiny chapel, or palace, covered with thousands upon thousands of sapphires; a meeting between the Arena Chapel and St Mark's basilica writ small and cheap. The blue sparkle was achieved by flooding the interior of the flat with 75,000 litres of copper sulphate solution. It did not take long for the bathtub, the walls, the floor and the ceiling to be taken over by a mesmerizing and menacing growth of gorgeous crystals. Nor did it take long for the pilgrims of blue to make the journey to 157 Harper Road. In keeping with the mythology of blue, *Seizure* is as foreboding as it is beautiful. Likewise, the liquid pools of milky turquoise approach the abject. Hiorns's council-flat palace, bejewelled with the grandeur, as well as the ill-omened fragments and liquidy rank of Venice, is today's equivalent of painting with light, not from lapis lazuli crystals, but from copper sulphate crystals.

Anna's mobile, like Hiorns's copper sulphate crystals (the child's science experiment of growing crystals grows out of control) grows and multiplies through the film. Born from the sugary shards of her daughter's blue sucker, the mobile operates as *the source*, not unlike those paintings of the same name by Ingres and Courbet.

The mobile crystallizes into the blue light that comes when Julie hears music. The mobile crystallizes into the blue pills that Julie fails to swallow in a suicide attempt. The mobile crystallizes into Julie's blue notes written with a blue pen on her late husband's score that is kept in a blue folder along with pictures of his mistress. The mobile crystallizes into the blue swimming pool that Julie swims in at night. The mobile crystallizes into the blue television image of bungee jumping on a programme that her mother with Alzheimer's has on but does not see.

Roger Hiorns, *Seizure* (blue detail), 2008, copper sulphate
crystals in a council flat, London, photograph.

Roger Hiorns, *Seizure* (coral red coat on blue detail), 2008, copper sulphate crystals in a council flat, London, photograph.

In a brilliant stroke of casting, Julie's mother who no longer remembers anything, who has forgotten her daughter, is played by Emmanuelle Riva, the star of *Hiroshima mon amour* (1959) and the famed character in the film by Alain Resnais and Marguerite Duras, who is so afraid of forgetting. In a sense, then, Julie, like me, also eats her blue mother. She is swallowed inside her, just as she was once inside her mother, just as Anna was once inside her.

From blue to blue. Such crystals of nucleic blue beauty, blue pain, blue memory, blue forgetting, blue childhood, blue old age, blue loss, blue sex, blue candy, blue music are 'fragments of the truth which attract to themselves, like a magnet, an inkling of the unknown'.[10]

18
'O BLUE'

NUMBERS AND LETTERS of the alphabet can be coloured by
the blues of synaesthesia, a 'disease' that plagued (or delighted)
such literary greats as Vladimir Nabokov. As Nabokov writes
of his 'colored hearing' in his autobiography, *Speak Memory*,
'Passing on to the blue group, there is a steely x, thunder-cloud
z, and huckleberry k'.[1] Rimbaud had the disease too, and wrote
a poem describing his coloured vowels: '*A noir, E blanc, I rouge,
U vert, O bleu: voyelles.* ('A black, E white, I red, U green, O blue:
vowels.']) Rimbaud sings a little ode to his blue, and croons in
old French, 'O blue'. *O* could be no other colour than blue.'

Blue skies and seas ensure the colour as all encompassing,
yet both the sky and the sea achieve their hue by the scattering
of (empty) light. 'Water is colorless, shallow water appears to
the color of whatever lies underneath it, but deep water is full
of this scattered light, the purer the water the deeper the blue'.[2]
Thereby, we might say that blue is as full as a large ornamental
'O', like those elaborately decorated letters at the start of a *Once-
upon-a-time* fairy tale. Yet blue is as empty as the number zero.
Julia Kristeva writes in 'Giotto's Joy', 'Colour is not zero meaning:
it is excess meaning'.[3]

GIOTTO'S O IS BLUE

Giotto is not only synonymous with blue; he is famous for his
perfect 'O'. Giorgio Vasari famously tells the story of 'Giotto's O'.
The artist was asked to demonstrate his artistic genius. He responded
by drawing a perfect circle freehand.

An island is circled by water. Utopia is not the island itself; it is
the blue between here and there. It is the blue all around. Perhaps

that is why Miró coloured the round island of his *Photo: ceci est la couleur de mes rêves* blue. Bluetopia.

LOOP

The Belgium-born Francis Alÿs, who lives and works in Mexico, made a radical, utopian gesture with his work entitled *Loop*:

> In 1997 he contributed to *InSite*, an exhibition held in the border region between San Diego, California, and Tijuana, Mexico. He used his commission fee to travel south from Tijuana, across to Australia, north up the Pacific Rim and south through Alaska, Canada, and the United States, reaching San Diego without having crossed the Mexico–US border. This . . . extravagant action . . . addressed the difficulties faced by Mexican citizens when trying to visit the US . . . As has been his custom, Alÿs disseminated this work through the postcard available to visitors here, spreading the ideas of the action to a global audience.[4]

Alÿs' *Loop* is the blue water that makes up the island of utopia (like Miró's *peinture-poésie*), which, in the words of Tim Robinson, is a 'land without shortcuts'.[5]

Like Yves Klein, Alÿs equates lines (national borders) with evil; colour is good. Colour, especially blue, as envisioned by Klein, did not set limits. As Nan Rosenthal writes, colour for Klein,

> means 'incommensurate space – space in which to liberate oneself . . . in certain works such as *Europe-Afrique*, 1961, Klein used color as though it could be an explicit and overtly political tool for ending wars, because if you paint a single color over a relief map of Western Europe and North Africa,

In order to go from Tijuana to San Diego without crossing the Mexico/United States border, I followed a perpendicular route away from the fence and circumnavigated the globe, heading 67° South East, North East and South East again until I reached my departure point. The project remained free and clear of all critical implications beyond the physical displacement of the artist.

Francis Alÿs, *Loop*, 1997, postcard.

you thereby eliminate the boundaries between countries with a unifying bath of blue.[6]

UtOpia loops blue.

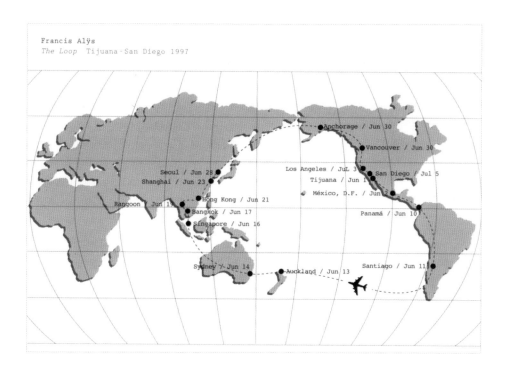

Francis Alÿs
The Loop Tijuana-San Diego 1997

Anchorage / Jun 30
Vancouver / Jun 30
Los Angeles / JuL 3 San Diego / Jul 5
Seoul / Jun 28   Tijuana / Jun 1
Shanghai / Jun 23   México, D.F. / Jun 2
Hong Kong / Jun 21
Rangoon   Jun 19   Panamá / Jun 10
Bangkok / Jun 17
Singapore / Jun 16
                                    Santiago / Jun 11
Sydney / Jun 14 Auckland / Jun 13

Francis Alÿs, *Loop*, 1997, postcard.

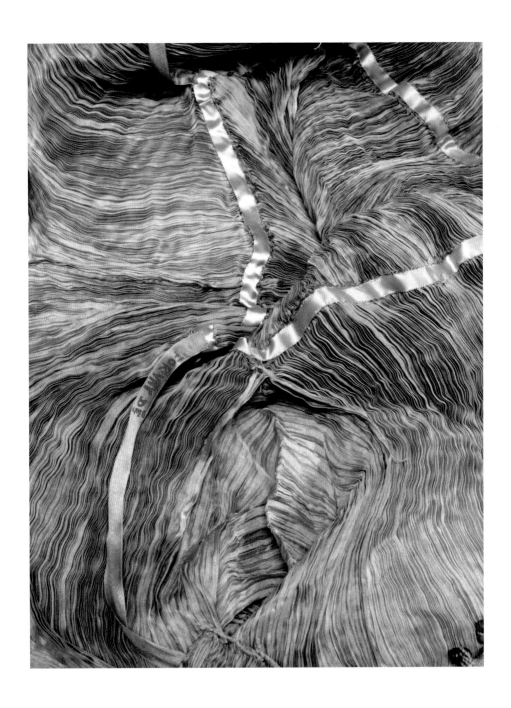

Wendy Ligon Smith, *Blue Fortuny Waves*, detail of Fortuny gown, 2011, photograph.

19
VENICE IS A WET MAP:
Tadzio is Blue

VENICE IS A SMALL and magical wet city. Venice is a blue
Fortuny dress of 117 folded islands. The shimmering folds of
Fortuny's Delphos gown reflect the city of water (Venice) from
which the dresses surfaced. In 1907 Fortuny created his first
Delphos, with its miniscule, glimmering waves of pleats, like the
water outside his palazzo in Venice. With only the slightest (yet
endless) variations, the famous folds of the Delphos would be
produced until his death in 1949. The Delphos pleats were probably
'put into the material when it was wet . . . under water, with
heat being applied later to ensure that . . . the folds remained
permanent'.[1] Today, the pleats from the original gowns still
miraculously hold. An everlasting fairy tale.

Born in Granada, the 'couturier who worked from memory'
moved to Venice when he was eighteen.[2] Fortuny was allergic to
horses. The city of water, through which one only travels by boat,
was a good answer to his illness.[3] A folding landscape[4] unfolds.

Not unlike the Proustian porcelain bowl in which little pieces
of paper become houses or people, Venice is a wet map, developing
like a cyanotype being washed.

In Venice you are always on water, on the way, intransitively
between here and there. Everything is wet in Venice and '[t]here
is [even] an especial type of Venetian risotto, more liquid than
elsewhere, that is known as *all'onda* or with the waves'.[5] Venice
is a big puddle.

Venice is not like other cities, since 'to reach some places you
must cross a bridge twice'.[6] Indeed, 'one is always going in circles.
It smells of cats'.[7] Water is the beauty of always sinking Venice,
but it is also its stinking olfaction, its abjection. In *Death in Venice*
(1912), Thomas Mann *abjects* his fairy-tale descriptions of Venice

with 'Asiatic cholera'. As is remarked in the film *Don't Look Now*, Venice is 'a city in aspic, left over from a dinner party where all the guests are dead and gone'.[8]

LOST IN VENICE

Venice is a labyrinth of a city, where one is always losing one's way, but is never really lost. Fittingly, Fortuny used a picture of a labyrinth as the icon for his first label, designed for his 'Knossos scarves'. The name 'Knossos' is an echo of the labyrinth that Theseus conquered with the same name. Likewise, Theseus' string, provided by Ariadne, is yet another metaphorical spool that glimmers with Fortuny's own threads stitched in the labyrinthine Venice.

DEATH IN VENICE IS LIKE A CYANOTYPE

When Thomas Mann's 'Gustav von Aschenbach' arrives in Venice, the experience is immediately theoretically utopian (as prescribed by such philosophers as Louis Marin, Fredric Jameson and Roland Barthes). To arrive in Venice is also to *not* arrive. In Mann's words, 'One had arrived and yet not arrived'.[9] Yet, Aschenbach (the fictional professor famous for his writing of that powerful tale entitled *A Study in Abjection*'[10]) feels that Venice 'would lead him back to where he had been, give him back to himself again'.[11] In the clutter of Venice, Aschenbach finds something that he did not know he was looking for, that is, the beautiful boy named Tadzio: 'With astonishment Aschenbach noticed that the boy was entirely beautiful'.[12] With astonishment, many of us, thanks to Gilbert Adair's fine *The Real Tadzio*, have learned that Tadzio was a 'real boy'. Born in 1900, the Polish boy named 'Władyslaw Moes', and nicknamed 'Adzio', was the 'sailor-suited ephebe'[13] who provoked that 'catastrophic loss of dignity suffered by a great and mature artist infatuated by a very much younger object of lust'.[14] But it must have been even more astonishing for Tadzio to discover (unbeknownst to him) that he had been Mann's boy-muse.

Mann's Tadzio, who wears 'the English sailor's suit . . . lanyards and bows and embroidery',[15] is not only a reverberation of the real 'Adzio', but is also a refrain of the sailor boys, as well as the Dionysian boys and St Sebastian boys pictured by the American photographer Fred Holland Day (1864–1933). Day was based in the Boston area but some of his most beautiful photographs were taken in the rocky, wild coastal area of Five Islands in Maine, where he ran something of an artist's colony for friends and fellow photographers. Also included, as a form of 'fresh air' social work, were children and adolescents of the immigrant and working class. The Constanza boys from a family of Italian immigrants were close to Day, and were often pictured. Day put cameras into the hands of the Constanzas (and other youths at Five Islands) as well. Mann and Day were contemporaries, separated by the Atlantic. Day took his photographs of beautiful boys at about the same time as Mann began writing of Aschenbach's gondola chasing after Tadzio's.

Alvin Langdon Coburn photographed Day wearing a theatrical long indoor wrap over a long gown (1900). Part of Day's extravagant personality was to present himself in various guises: 'a sailor, a North African sheik . . . a black magician . . . Christ'.[16] Day liked costumes. Here, his costume appears spiritual and from another time. The image is composed of very dark sepia tones, with creamy light emerging, not unlike Caravaggio's *Narcissus* (1597–9). Day's imagery can be described as the 'overwrought . . . emotionalism of Caravaggio' through the lens of the 'more placid moves of his contemporaries', like the painter 'Hippolyte Flandrin'.[17] Day is posed pulling open a curtain; he is performing the exiting of a photographic darkroom. On his right hand he wears a large ring.

Fred Holland Day, *Nude Youth in Rocky Landscape, c.* 1905, photograph, cyanotype.

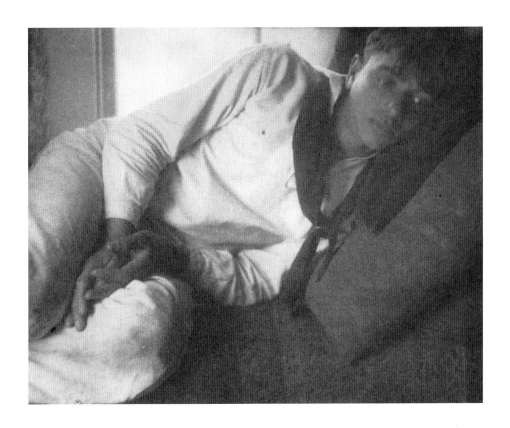

Fred Holland Day, *Tony Constanza in Sailor Suit*, photograph, cyanotype.

He is looking directly at the camera. He has a Van Dyck beard. The image has a Gothic appeal. Something Mary Shelley about it. And a little Johnny Depp. Supernatural. At his feet are four photographic trays of chemicals that appear like stones on a pathway. Day's baths of magical waters are puddles at his feet, not unlike the women wearing their mermaid-like Delphos gowns with fish-tail 'puddles around their feet'. In his puddles, like the reflecting (*photo*-graphic) waters of Caravaggio's *Narcissus*, the beautiful faces of young boys would surface.[18]

Aschenbach drifts (cruises) along the canals in a bobbing black gondola. Aschenbach follows Tadzio, not only like Scotty follows Madeleine in *Vertigo*, or like Proust's Narrator follows Albertine, or like Akerman's (Marcel-like) Simon follows the (Albertine-like) Ariane, but, perhaps, especially like Roland Barthes cruises for readers in The *Pleasure of the Text*: 'I must seek out this reader (must 'cruise' him) *without knowing where he is.*'[19]

Like Dionysus, perhaps like all beautiful adolescent boys who reside between childhood and adulthood, Tadzio is feminine in appearance. Tadzio is described as St Sebastian. Tadzio is like Day's photographs of St Sebastian. Tadzio is Day's cyanotype boy in a sailor suit. (Although made from a photographic negative, Day is using the same type of exposure process as Anna Atkins and Annabel Dover.)

In the 1911 cyanotype, Day wears a sailor suit too, along with Maynard White, the son of photographer Clarence White. Day is caught strangely gazing at the doppelgänger sailor-suited boy beside him: the doubling undoes. The borders are abjectly breached between man and boy. As Kristeva explains, 'it is . . . not lack of cleanliness or health that causes abjection but what disturbs identity, system, order. What does not respect borders, positions, rules. The in-between, the ambiguous, the composite.'[20]

Referring to the cyanotypes of 'Mississippi Blues' made by the American photographer Henry Bosse, whose project was to *map*[21] the boggy river, like Hokusai's Prussian blue on white prints

Fred Holland Day, *F. Holland Day and Maynard*, 1911, photograph, cyanotype.

Henry Bosse, *Wagon Bridge at Fulton, Illinois*, 1889, photograph, cyanotype.

of *Thirty-Six Views of Mount Fuji*,[22] Rebecca Solnit writes that 'you arrive in this world where darkness and light are blue and white, where bridges and people and apples are blue as lakes, as though everything were seen through the melancholy atmosphere that here is cyanide'.[23] These blues, like the encroaching, often flooding waters of the Mississippi river, do not respect borders. Everything is blue. In Bosse's 1889 *Wagon Bridge at Fulton, Illinois*, 'a blue oval' floats on the page 'like a bubble'.[24] Even the border around the blue egg is dappled with blue shapes, like Proust's 'little pieces of paper become houses or people'.[25]

Likewise, Venice is borderless: 'it is a place of doubleness, and perhaps therefore of duplicity and double standards'.[26] Looking at Venice as reflected in its waterways, sea and lagoons, 'Venice seems to have no foundation except for reflections. Only its reflections are visible. Venice and Venice's image are inseparable'.[27] (Like Narcissus and his reflection, like Day and Maynard White as blue echoes.)

TADZIO IS BLUE

'A longing for nothingness.'[28] Is this not, as Aschenbach wonders in *Death in Venice*, the most perfect form of desire? If blue is the light that got lost, is nothing, then blue is the most pure form of desire. Tadzio walks as if he were made of light, like a Fred Holland Day photograph. Aschenbach discovers beauty in the form of Tadzio (he wants nothing more than to be 'on this island with this beautiful boy'[29]), and abjection, in the form of the smell of 'Asiatic cholera' all at once.

At the end of the novel, Aschenbach and Tadzio are amongst the few left on the beach. Through the grey twilight of his eyes, Aschenbach is watching Tadzio becoming one with the blue Venetian sea. An abandoned camera, with its anthropomorphic leggy tripod, has been left on the beach. Aschenbach is becoming inseparable from the image of Tadzio as Venice, as is metaphorically suggested by the figure of the camera on the beach. In the words of Mann, 'An autumnal, out-of-season air seemed to hover over the once so colourful and populous resort, now almost deserted, with litter left about on the sand. An apparently abandoned camera stood on its tripod at the edge of the sea. And the black cloth over it fluttered and flapped in the freshening breeze'.[30]

Aschenbach is watching Tadzio walking into the sea. As Tadzio becomes one with the water, he shoots a glance back at Aschenbach. Aschenbach is ill, yet this look fills him to the brim with abject pleasure. The image dissolves into Day's Venetian blue and cerulean blue cyanotype *Nude Youth in Rocky Landscape, circa* 1905, where water, blue and boy are inseparable. Waterblueboy.

Aschenbach (through the aspic lens of Kristeva) can be understood as abjecting himself with the same motion through which he claims to establish himself. In the process of becoming an other at the expense of his own death, Aschenbach changes. A metamorphosis takes place, in which he gives birth to himself amidst the stench of Venice and the smell of death. Smell, unlike vision, seeps through boundaries, cannot be walled off. Likewise (as stated in the chapter 'A Foggy Lullaby'), blue is apprehensible, yet invisible (it is nothing). Blue shares something with olfaction. And olfaction is closely connected to abjection.

Aschenbach 'abreacts'.[31] Aschenbach abjects. He becomes his own book on abjection. Now, in 'the twilight [morning / mourning light] of the immeasurable',[32] Aschenbach is no longer separate from other things. Nothing is missing. There is nothing to be found. He is as limitless, as abject, as the colour blue.

20
Domestic Blues:
Agnès Varda's *Le Bonheur*

THE DOMESTIC 'BLUES' of Agnès Varda's film *Le Bonheur* (1965) speak a voice of paradoxical 'troubled light' (Goethe)[1] that is feminine and feminist. In Varda's *Le Bonheur* you hear blue laughing and sobbing as the timbre of the two (mostly silent) women of the film: a wife named 'Thérèse' and a lover named 'Émilie'.

Colour, as *voiced* and *envisioned* by Varda, forms a particular *timbre* of blue, which embowers the word *miss*:

1. As in to go wrong; to fail; to not be *in time*. 'Just missed'.
2. An absent person or pet or object can go missing.
3. When we long for someone we *miss* them.

In Varda's hands, 'missing' sounds 'blue'.

VARDA'S *LE BONHEUR* LOOPS BLUE

When Varda went back to the town where *Le Bonheur* was filmed and asked various residents, 'What is happiness?'– a question that is necessarily at the heart of utopian thought– the young man who teaches swimming claims, while standing in front of a below-ground window, which gives an enchanted view to the pool behind him, full of turquoise-blue water and dolphinesque swimmers, 'For me happiness is warmth, the memory of *maman*'s tummy, water'.[2] Like a swimmer taking laps, utopia loops blue.

In Varda's *Le Bonheur*, there is a comprehensive narrative: a man named François is perfectly in love with his wife – quiet,

pretty, buxom Thérèse, mother of his deliciously sweet children. (Of note here is the fact that the two actors were and still are married in 'real life' and even the two adorable children are their own offspring.[3]) Trouble erupts when François meets another beautiful woman (Émilie), a quiet postal worker suited in official blue, who sells blue stamps.

While in the post office, a *timbre* (a stamp) with a blue Chagall painting of a wedding couple appears in the blue post office. Émilie, the very pretty postal worker, dressed in her blue uniform, offers the *timbre* up to François and viewers alike. (Yves Klein's blue *timbre* is heard again.[4]) Here the mood is a happy blue, yet we feel sad and even angry knowing that Thérèse is home cooking, sewing, minding, nesting.

Agnès Varda, *Le Bonheur*, 1965.

158

Nesting

If only I hadn't minded, I used to say, but I did mind very much.
I minded more than very much. I minded more than I could ever
have dared. Mind the door. Mind the glass. Mind the fire. Mind the
child. I never minded the warmth. I minded the need. It was needed
to have minded, I used to say, but was it needed to have minded
more than very much? More than I could ever have dared?

Voice-over from the film, *Riddles of the Sphinx* (1977)
by Laura Mulvey and Peter Wollen

Yet, we might say that Thérèse is there in the post office, she is merely (as Mary Kelly has remarked of our cultural distancing of the maternal body) 'too close to see'.[5]

Émilie is a repeat of Thérèse, perhaps a bit sexier in her child-less state, but just as quiet. It is summer. In loving both women, François finds himself to be really, really 'happy'. On a picnic with their perfect and beautiful little family, Thérèse wants to know why François has been so happy lately. Not wanting to lie, he confesses his affair with Émilie. He explains that he is full of love. He tells her that he has enough good love for both of them. Thérèse says little. Thérèse accepts. Thérèse says nothing, really. But during a post-coital nap out in the countryside, Thérèse slips away and drowns in a nearby lake. Perhaps it is an aggressive suicide, or perhaps, like Ophelia, more of a slip while picking flowers and an opportunity to let the water do the work.[6] François finds Thérèse in her blue dress. Varda loops this small blue piece of film over again and again. (She loops it blue.) This is the only loop in the film. It is hard to get your mind around what is happening, what has happened.

Thérèse is a believer, without cynicism (even if the same could not be said for Varda). Thérèse is a pure innocent *martyred* to the promise of happiness in the form of marriage. Despite all the flowers that appear in *Le Bonheur*, Thérèse is, perhaps, closer to Paul Delaroche's painting of a *Young Christian Martyr* (1855) than she is to Millais's *Ophelia*. At the outset, the martyrs of

Delaroche and Varda are very different, even beyond period and medium. Delaroche has pictured his maiden, with her Fortuny-like gown floating in the water, as all victim: her helpless arms are tied by ropes. The water and the setting of the painting are dark ('*gloomth*'). Only in death will Delaroche's fairy-tale girl live happily ever after. But the true focus of this painting is brighter (like Thérèse): it is the loop of gold that lights the young martyr's face like a camera's flash. As Stephen Bann remarks, 'the plastic use that Delaroche makes of the halo has few parallels in his own work or in that of his contemporaries'.[7] It keeps her going round and round. It even lights the water and parts of her chrysalis-like dress into a range of ('opalescent'[8]) Polaroid-blues. Like Varda. Delaroche loops his fair maiden too.

In *Le Bonheur*, I am bothered by the yellow-green algae that smatters the lake. I am reminded of the 1937 painting of Ophelia by the Surrealist painter André Masson: 'Ophelia has fallen into a stagnant pool where reeds poking through a layer of algae will soon close over her . . . Her mouth is open as she sings. She is adorned with a flower garland ("crow-flowers, nettles, daisies, and long purples") and a daisy in place of her eye, flowers symbolic of her madness'.[9]

The yellow algae on Varda's lake and in Masson's *Ophelia* takes me further into yellow madness, and that of the yellow madness of Charlotte Perkins Gilman's 1892 short story 'The Yellow Wallpaper' ('yellow things . . . not beautiful ones like buttercups, but old foul, bad yellow things').[10] I sink into the madness of Van Gogh's yellow 'meat-eating sunflowers'.[11] Indeed, Varda's own sunflowers are mad too, as they dance throughout the film, from beginning to end, to the dramas of Mozart. In 'The Yellow Wallpaper', yellow seeps through barriers and smells like sulphur and creeps throughout the house. In *Le Bonheur*, yellow penetrates past barriers and sounds like Mozart and grows fast and unnervingly large, like summer sunflowers.

Paul Delaroche, *Young Christian Martyr,* 1855, oil on canvas.

After Thérèse's death, François mourns her a little. Then, he abruptly marries Émilie. The colours and the time of the film switch to fall. Now the little family has a mother and wife again. They are no longer blue. Nor red. They are all wearing yellow. They are supposed to be happy. Or are they?

In *Le Bonheur* you can hear colour laughing, sobbing, screaming, peddling its non-sense. It is the voice, the timbre of the mostly silent women of the film. Entire scenes are carefully staged with an emphasis on a single colour: blue, yellow, red, green. It is colour-field painting turned film. Yet the colours are both carefully and anarchically chosen. Patterns of meaning are set and then are destroyed. At first, we read the colours as though they have been perpetuated by cultural myths: blue is good, the Virgin, the maternal and the lovely wife. Thérèse wears it well. But that myth is usurped when Émilie, the childless homewrecker, is also cast in blue. We feel Thérèse's loss. We feel Émilie's loss. We hear the blues. Varda uses colour to shatter meaning.

BLUE PROMISE

> *He promised to buy me a pair of blue stockings, A pair of blue garters that cost him but two pence, He promis'd to buy me a bunch of blue ribbons, To tie up my bonny brown hair.*
> 'What Can the Matter Be?', traditional nursery rhyme, late 1700s

Thérèse is a seamstress who works from home. Thérèse's husband François is a joiner. Together, they both labour at stitching together, joining together.

At the beginning of the film, the little family is on a picnic in the woods. They walk to the nearby park. Thérèse is picking flowers. Over the bridge of the lake, the body of blue and yellow water that Thérèse will later drown in on a future 'happy' day, walks a pregnant, modern *Madonna del parto*, dressed in blue, the promise of blue.

Later, around a large dining table in the garden, Thérèse, François and another family of friends celebrate the birth of a baby girl. (The 'table' is an object that Sara Ahmed circles in her book, *The Promise of Happiness*, as the locus of family happiness.[12]) The scene is all summer, flowers, rosy-cheeked children, delicious food, wine and the new mother's ample breasts dripping with milk.

But the promise of happiness fails. Happiness goes missing. Happiness gets lost. Matrimonial happiness is a mythology, is a paradox, and is hued blue.

After Thérèse's death, François and the adults of the family meet around another family table. They are there to set a table of happiness for the children's future. Who will take these delicious children? Should they be separated? No, they should not be separated and they should stay with François. They should stay together. Émilie is the future mother phantom at this table. But most of us will not see her yet. Nevertheless, again in the words of Mary Kelly, '[s]he is there, she is just too close to see'. Thérèse is missing, is blue. Just as she was when she had drowned in the algae-covered lake and François circled the area asking, 'Have you seen a woman in a blue dress?' Blue, writes William Gass, is the colour 'of everything that's empty'.[13]

'For Blue', claims Derek Jarman, 'there are no boundaries or solutions'.[14]

NOTHING BUT A THIN LAYER OF COLOUR

As in Giotto's Arena Chapel, Varda gives the viewer a second stage of signification: the colour. *Le Bonheur* was Varda's first film in colour.

Varda's blue 'happiness' works like Giotto's blue 'joy'. Just as in the Arena Chapel, when the two angels famously and abruptly tear back the Chapel's layer of blue to reveal a field of pure red. It turns out the blue heaven, as unveiled by the hands of Giotto's angels, is 'nothing but a thin layer of color'; Varda reveals happiness and marriage as 'nothing but a thin layer of color'.[15]

21

ARAN IS A BLUE PLACE WHERE IT IS HARD TO FIND ANYTHING MISSING

THE YEAR IS 1962.

It is the American painter Patricia Patterson's first year on Inis Mór, the largest of the three Aran islands off of the West Coast of Ireland. Inis Mór is the biggest of the three tiny islands that 'lie in a line across the mouth of Galway Bay'[1] and make up Aran. 'Three wastes of rock'.[2] All three islands (Inis Mór, Inis Meáin and Inis Oírr)[3] are friends with frequent and violent damaging storms that guarantee their barrenness, and their cragginess that is shaped by every slam of wind and wave.

Patterson is beautiful and she is eighteen years old. It was John Synge's book on the Aran Islands that had started her adolescent dreaming of these 'three wastes of rock'. She found a room of her own, which made the dreaming real, on the island of Inis Mór, where she discovered friends, who were like family. Nan, Cóilín, Pat, Mary and a dog named Jigs.

In a 1962 photograph, taken by Alen MacWeeney, we see the girl in the year of her arrival. Patterson's youth and elation bursts from her tightly buttoned cardigan and her white Peter Pan collar. You can *hear* the stone walls behind her, plotting and plotting and plotting. The 7,000-mile lacework of walls, themselves built upon a *non-land* of grey flint (with hardly any soil, nearly treeless). A place 'where stone is stone and is not polished'.[4]

The hard-hearted stones of Inis Mór cannot suppress Patterson's happiness, although they do appear grave, like the remains of an archaeological dig. When Tim Robinson describes Inis Mór as a 'knot of stone from which the sky has broken out', he could also be describing Patterson in this exuberant photograph. Here, Patterson with her arms hugging her sides, clasps her hands together in what is perhaps a necessary gesture to ground her. Nan so kindly smiles, as she peers in between Patterson and Cóilín. Cóilín pulls us in with his heavy-browed gaze. Surely he hears the loud silence of Patricia's pure joy. He cracks a smile.

Air service to the Aran Islands did not begin until 1970. Electricity did not come until 1976. Aran is still a very remote place. It is still rather hard to get to. Tourism and new ferries did not come until the 1980s. Nevertheless, what happened five hundred years ago in Aran is spoken with presentness: 'chronology here', in the spirit of u-topia's u-chronos, 'fades away like tobacco smoke from the next tale'.[5]

In Patterson's voice, one hears a small rustle of Irish. Hers is a neither-nor voice; a voice that she carried back and forth from her trips to Aran, from 1962 to 1989. Nearly every year. Sometimes staying more than a year.

The 'grain' of Patterson's voice is vermilion, like the vermil- lion-orange that threatens to colour the whiteness of Irish skin, like the vermilion-orange that Patterson uses as underpainting to sketch *Cóilín Smoking, Pat Reading, Mary Washing Up, The Rabbit and the Kiss* and *Pat and Mary Skinning Rabbits.* In the latter, the table is not the scene of the promise of family and happiness. Hardly a child in Patterson's *oeuvre* – but plenty of dead rabbits waiting to be skinned.

In the years during which Patricia lived in and visited Aran, the surprising colours of the interiors of the homes were anarchi- cally chosen, as if sparring with speech. When something looked 'woebegone', whether a wall, a shelf, a door, a window frame, a breakfront, a picture frame or almost anything at all, it was fresh- ened by a new coat of paint. The can of paint is used with careful oxymoronic arbitrariness, until it is empty. As Patterson writes in her essay 'Aran Kitchens, Sweaters', published in 1978 in the journal *Heresies*, 'the unpredictable color patches create a liveliness and variety in a house made up of white and two colors. But what colors! A kelly green and chrome yellow used in equal amounts . . . It's an anarchistic way to paint'.[6]

Patricia Patterson, *Cóilín Smoking, Pat Reading, Mary Washing Up*, 1982.

Patricia Patterson, *Pat and Mary Skinning Rabbits.*

And while, at that time, the men wore colours that matched the greys and browns of the 'awesome' stoneyard of Aran, the women dressed colourfully against the rocks of Aran.[7]

NOT SO BLUE

It has cleared, and the sun is shining with a luminous warmth that makes the whole island glisten with the splendor of a gem, and fills the sea and sky with a radiance of blue light.

John Synge, *The Aran Islands*

Nevertheless, the blueness of Aran is only a sometimes affair. While one can find, as John Synge once did, that 'the sun is shining with a luminous warmth that makes the whole island glisten with the splendour of a gem, and fills the sea and sky with a radiance of blue light',[8] such cerulean splendour is not the rule of an Aran day, no matter what the season.

Fair Aran is fickle. Grey Aran is stable. A grey storm is always ready to rise, unexpectedly, quickly. Blue, in the hands of Patterson (and John Synge), is the colour that, at least when the light is right and the weather cooperates, nearly swallows up the tiny islands of Aran. 'Blue will swallow . . . like a bell swallows silence'.[9]

I asked Máiréad Robinson,[10] 'What is blue on Aran that is not sky or sea?' She paused. She thought. And then she sat upright with great joy to describe the blue gentians that appear on the island in March and April, and spoke of 'sheets of sapphires . . . magical blue flowers'. Perhaps, then, these gentians are the only blue on Aran that is not of the sky, not of the sea, not of the grey rock. These magical flowers, these blue bells of Aran, come out overnight, as if one were hallucinating, and last only a fortnight.

Even on a bright blue day, the island remains grey at its stone heart. (Again, as Tim Robinson describes Inis Mór like a 'knot of stone from which the sky has broken out'.) Grey rules the day.

Johannes Vermeer, *Woman Reading a Letter*, c. 1662–3, oil on canvas.

Aran blues know that their very livelihood (their cerulean, ultramarine skies and oceans, their sheets of magical sapphire of blue gentians) is dependent on Aran's relentless greys. Like Vermeer's blues, as in his painting *Woman Reading a Letter* (1662–3), the blues achieve their vividness through the nearby greys. The grey skirt of Vermeer's woman makes her blue smock that much more blue, just as the grey stones of Aran make the Irish sea that much more blue.

'SHALLOW-BOX FRAMING'

In 1977, Patterson published an essay with her husband, the late film critic and painter Manny Farber, on Chantal Akerman's 1975 film, *Jeanne Dielman, 23 Quai du Commerce, 1080 Bruxelles*. The title of the essay is 'Kitchen Without Kitsch'. In a glance, one can see the influence (or perhaps only a strong, unconscious coincidence) of the Dielman interior on Patterson's own kitchen scenes. In describing the film, Patterson and Farber comment on 'the integrity of things as they already stand'[11] or on the 'perfect mathematical inhale-exhale clarity',[12] lines that easily also evoke Patterson's paintings, especially her clean *Cóilín Smoking, Pat Reading, Mary Washing Up.*

In Akerman's own words on the shooting of *Jeanne Dielman*, 'I didn't get too close, but I didn't get too far away'.[13] Patterson's own not too close, not too far away approach to the interiors of Aran echoes Akerman's 'shallow-box framing' and 'respectful' distance.[14] For both, this middle distance is filmic and lends an ear to the Roland Barthesian 'middle voice'.

Akerman's 'drama of the kitchen routine'[15] makes handsome use of a powerful (with)holding, much like Patricia's work. Patricia holds time still with her breathless short sentences as paintings, just as Akerman holds time still through her singular, long sentence of a film for 201 long minutes. Jeanne Dielman's kitchen drama and that of Patricia's are both like Aran itself, which is 'full of its own angry power, but oddly calm and flat, like something held down, contained but swelling'.[16]

WRITING ALOUD

> *To be listening is to be inclined toward the opening of meaning,*
> *hence to a slash, a cut in un-sensed indifference.*
>
> Jean-Luc Nancy

The immediacy of Patricia's paintings, their plainspoken beauty, has the effect of reading a beautiful letter aloud. For years, Patricia has recorded the voices of those she knew in Aran, either on tape or through written notes, as well as saving their letters that came through the post. She saves. She records. She takes notes. She studies the language – not only the Irish, but also the creases, the doubling-up of the Irish English and the British English, which open out in the utterances of the Aran people. In working between various forms of English, their speech always sounds, according to Patterson, translated. Nevertheless, if we listen carefully, what we hear is that which is, in fact, untranslatable. (Aran winds colour their speech.)

Patterson finds great beauty in the steadfastness of this language that in English is still Irish. In her installation *Here and There, Back and Forth*, she provides a handsomely written letter from her friend Mary, writ large as a painting. The scale of the letters and the beauty of the drawing of the letter give the affect of writing aloud. Barthes describes 'writing aloud' as 'a text where we can hear the grain of the throat, the patina of consonants . . . A certain singing can give an idea of this vocal writing'.[17] The folk songs of Western Ireland are inseparable from the rhythm and the twists and turns of Aran speech. Like the blues of the American South, Aran song too is riddled with its own forms of 'bent notes' and 'worried notes'.

In her letter from her friend Mary writ larger, writ aloud as art, Patterson provides just the postscript – the rest of the letter is *missing*.

P.S. I must tell you about the dog. We are very sad and lonely after him. He had a habit of chasing back to Onaght and Bungowla for seven or eight years. What he died of we don't know, it might have been poison. He wasn't able to make it home. I would feel better if he had come home to die with us. Mary Dírrane saw him. She said he looked very breathless with his tongue out. I went back [to] the road trying to find him and I couldn't. They said over there that he died in the fields. The saddest part is that he must have suffered for three or four days. The house is so lonely without him. The 28th of August he went.

Aran is a place where it is hard to find anything missing with its big high walls. People are better off who have no pets. So goodbye, hoping to hear from you soon. In a hurry for the post.

Mary

Aran, Mary tells us, is a place where it is hard to find anything missing. We know what she means. It is a place of high walls that make mobility and careful searching difficult. But to say that Aran is a place where it is hard to find anything missing is also to suggest its perfection. One does not miss on Aran, for it is all there, at least all that we need. In the words of Colm Tóibín, 'Here is enough'.[18]

Mary's postscript is a paradox, like the colour blue.

MUST ....
VERY SAD AND LONELY AFTER HIM.
A HABIT OF CHASING BACK TO ON-
D BUNGOWLA FOR SEVEN OR
EARS. WHAT HE DIED OF WE DON'T
MIGHT HAVE BEEN POISON. HE
ABLE TO MAKE IT HOME. I WOULD
TTER IF HE HAD COME HOME TO
H US. MARY DIRRANE SAW HIM.
HE LOOKED VERY BREATHLESS WITH
GUE OUT. I WENT BACK THE ROAD
TO FIND HIM AND I COULDN'T. THEY SAID

HERE THAT HE DIED IN THE FIELDS.
EST PART IS THAT HE MUST HAVE SUFFERED
E OR FOUR DAYS. THE HOUSE IS SO
WITHOUT HIM. THE 28TH OF AUGUST
T.

AN IS A PLACE WHERE IT IS HARD
D ANYTHING MISSING WITH ITS
IGH WALLS. PEOPLE ARE BETTER
WHO HAVE NO PETS. SO GOODBYE,
G TO HEAR FROM YOU SOON, IN
RRY FOR THE POST.

Patricia Patterson, Letter, from the installation *Here and There, Back and Forth*.

Henri Matisse, *Polynésie, la mer,* 1946, gouache on paper cutout.

In Lieu of a Blue Ending:
Un-knitting a Cerulean Jumper

At the very beginning Thomas More designated utopia as a
place, an island in the distant South Seas . . . but I am not there.

Ernst Bloch, '*Something's Missing*'

UTOPIA

Like Joan Miró's 1925 little blue island that I cannot let go of,
that sits in a sea of white in his 1925 *Photo: This is the color of*
my dreams – the word *utopia* has a feeling for the sound of 'O'.
'O' circles around the island 'O' of utopia, which is squatted in
the middle of a little ocean of less vocal letters. But I am not there.

The ocean goes all around utopia. On the day of his arrival
on the two by nine mile island of Inis Mór, Tim Robinson (Ireland's
Proust) was 'met by an old man who explained the basic geography'.
'The ocean goes all around the island', he said.[1]

OU-TOPIA

The word 'utopia' was first coined as a noun (a proper noun),
a place name in Thomas More's novel *Utopia* (1516). Islands
often set the stage of utopias, which are watery by nature. Utopias
are 'thalasso-graphic',[2] from the Greek *thalassa*, meaning 'sea'–
a word that I have already used to describe the condition of the
cyanotype. Utopias are sea-writing. Sea-writing has an emphasis
on going round, in finding the round and living the round.
Matisse drew it with scissors. Although a rectangular square,
Matisse's *Polynesia, the Sea* (1946) has a round feeling. It floats.

Francis Alÿs, *Fairy Tales*, 1995, photograph (detail from performance piece).

Tall squares of grey-blue-green-turquoise and deep ultramarine blue give way to cutouts of white shapes which soar over the contrasting blues. White silhouettes that suggest birds, coral, fish, sea anemone, small sharks, seaweed and jellyfish hover in a blue world that is neither sky nor sea, but both.

My approach to the island of utopia sails on the ship of the great utopian writer Louis Marin (1931–1992).[3] Between shores, utopia is contradictory; it never loses sight of dystopia. Unfinished, like Miró's *Photo* appears to be (even if it is not), the approach to utopia is always already a turning back. It *loops*.

EU-TOPIA

This concept of unfinished work may sound 'dystopic', but in the hands of some utopian thinkers (like Ernst Bloch, Louis Marin, Roland Barthes and Thomas More) this is labour at its happiest. Hellenists now, and in 1516, when More first coined the term 'utopia' as both the subject and title of his little book, understand that the word is a fusion of the Greek adverb *ou*, meaning 'not', with the noun *topos*, which means 'place'. The etymology of utopia is 'not a place'. Likewise, Hellenists understand that the word 'utopia' is also punning on another Greek compound: *eutopia*, which means 'happy' or 'fortunate' place. Like the happy-sad sense of the colour blue, the sound of the word 'utopia' sounds like 'not a place' and 'happy place' at once. This blue paradox is underscored by the fact that we hear More's *Utopia* through the voice of an explorer-narrator named 'Hythloday', which is a Greek compound that signifies 'nonsense peddler'.[4]

Utopia is a nowhere island, yet we keep trying to get there. It is always unfinished. Fredric Jameson likens utopia's always-already unfinished essence with the 'pleasures of construction' found in 'the garage workshop, of the home mechanic erector sets, of Lego, of bricolating and cobbling together things of all kinds . . .

in a never-ending variation fed by new ideas and information . . .
these utopian constructions convey the spirit of non-alienated
labour and production'.[5] Jameson's utopias, without an end in
sight, are hopeful in that which Barthes identifies as radical,
'successful idleness', or good laziness. In his inspiring interview
entitled 'Dare to be Lazy', Barthes *bricolates* on knitting:

> Perhaps the most unconventional and thus the most literally
> scandalous thing I ever saw in my life – scandalous for the
> people watching, not for me – was a young man seated in a
> subway car in Paris who pulled some knitting out of his bag
> and openly began to knit. Everyone felt scandalized, but no
> one said anything.
>
> Now, knitting is the perfect example of a manual activity
> that is minimal, gratuitous, without finality, but that still
> represents a beautiful and successful idleness.[6]

Francis Alÿs took it one step further with his Fairy Tale 'action',
as he walked through Stockholm whilst unravelling behind him
the blue sweater that he was wearing, to make a trail not of pebbles
or breadcrumbs, but of yarn. Alÿs spins his own yarn on the
'action' when he comments that 'in Stockholm, once the walk was
done and the sweater unravelled I retraced my steps to document
the journey, following the long blue thread on the street and in
the park. Midway back I ran into this old lady who was patiently
rolling a blue yarn under her arm, carefully gathering up the wool
of my unravelled sweater – maybe to knit a similar one at home.'[7]
Like *Blue Mythologies*, Alÿs is a man who knits (unknits) out of
the blue.

*Blue, spontaneous and fragile, so wide-spread that
I may draw deep from the well of illusion and
accept that I am beside a lake, or a field of blue flax
in flower . . .*

Colette

REFERENCES

INTRODUCTION: *PARADOXICALLY BLUE*

1 Significant for *Blue Mythologies* is the fact that Barthes cut his writing
  teeth (as an essayist who embraces the novelesque) on Marcel Proust's *In
  Search of Lost Time.* Not to be overlooked is the fact that Proust's *Search*
  began as a series of literary essays (criticism) and became peculiarly
  modern: something that was neither philosophy nor novel. As he notably
  questioned of himself: 'Should I make it a novel, or a philosophical study
  – am I a novelist?' (Marcel Proust, from the *Carnet de 1908*). The
  quotation can be found in the introduction to *Marcel Proust: On Art
  and Literature, 1896–1919,* translated by Sylvia Townsend Warner,
  with an introduction by Terence Kilmartin (New York, 1984), p. 11.
  Or as Barthes later put it: 'It must all be considered as if spoken by a
  character in a novel' (Roland Barthes, *Roland Barthes by Roland Barthes,*
  trans. Richard Howard, New York, 1977, from an epigraph at the
  beginning of the book, unpaginated).
2 Colette, *For a Flower Album,* trans. Roger Senhouse (New York, 1959),
  p. 36.
3 James Clifford, 'On Ethnographic Allegory', in *Writing and Culture:
  The Poetics and Politics of Ethnography*, ed. James Clifford and George
  Marcus (Berkeley, CA, 1986), p. 121.
4 *The Wordsworth Dictionary of Phrase and Fable,* based on the original
  book by E. C. Brewer (London, 2006), p. 151.
5 As explained to me by Dr Peter N. Burns, Professor and Chair,
  Department of Medical Biophysics, University of Toronto.
6 Barthes, Preface to the 1970 edition of *Mythologies,* trans. Annette Lavers
  (London, 2000), p. 9.
7 Hayden White, from a comment that he made during the conference
  held in tribute to his work entitled 'Between History and Narrative:
  Colloquium in Honor of Hayden White', University of Rochester, 2009.
8 William T. Cooper, *The Birds of Paradise and Bower Birds* (Sydney, 1977),
  p. 266.
9 Paul Spencer-Longhurst, *The Blue Bower, Rossetti in the 1860s*
  (Birmingham, 2000), p. 50.
10 Spencer-Longhurst, *The Blue Bower,* p. 50.

1 EVERYTHING IS BLUE

1 Jean Cocteau, 'Plain Song' ('Plain-chant'), in *Modern French Poets: Selections with Translations, Dual-Language Book,* ed. Wallace Fowlie (New York,, 1993), p. 131.
2 Rebecca Solnit, *A Field Guide to Getting Lost* (New York and London 2005), p. 29.
3 William Gass, *On Being Blue: A Philosophical Inquiry* (David R. Godine: Jaffrey, NH, 1997), p. 34.
4 Michel Pastoureau, *Blue: The History of a Color*, trans. Markus I. Cruse (Princeton, NJ, 2001), p. 179.
5 Gabriel García Márquez, *Love in the Time of Cholera*, trans. Edith Grossman (New York, 1997), p. 114.
6 Marie Darrieusecq, *Breathing Underwater*, trans. Linda Coverdale (London, 2002), p. 103.
7 Solnit, *A Field* Guide, p. 29.

2 BLUE IS JOYFUL-SAD

1 Julia Kristeva, 'Giotto's Joy' in *Desire in Language: A Semiotic Approach to Literature and Art,* ed. Leon S. Roudiez, trans. Thomas Gora, Alice Jardine and Leon S. Roudiez (New York, 1980), p. 224.
2 Ibid., p. 223.
3 Marcel Proust, *In Search of Lost Time,* trans. C. K. Scott-Moncrieff and Terence Kilmartin, revd. D. J. Enright, vol. v, *The Captive* and *The Fugitive* (New York, 1993), p. 877.
4 Richard Offner, 'Giotto, Non-Giotto', in *Giotto: The Arena Chapel Frescoes*, ed. James Stubblebine (New York and London, 1995), p. 135.
5 As Proust writes about these same angels: 'I had the same impression of actual movement, literally real activity . . . winged creatures of a particular species that had really existed . . . real creatures with a genuine power of flight . . . "looping the loop". . . reminiscent of . . . young pupils of Garros practising gliding'. *In Search of Lost Time*, v, *The Captive* and *The Fugitive*, pp. 878–9.
6 Proust, *In Search of Lost Time*, v, *The Captive* and *The Fugitive*, p. 879.
7 Rotraut Uecker, artist and widow of Yves Klein, as quoted in Thomas McEvilley, 'Yves Klein: Conquistador of the Void', *Yves Klein, 1928–1962: A Retrospective* (New York, 1982), p. 62.
8 Helmut Newton, *Pola Woman* (Munich, 1992), p. 10.
9 Roland Barthes, describing Robert Mapplethorpe's *Young Man with Arm Extended*, in his *Camera Lucida: Reflections on Photography*, trans. Richard Howard (New York, 1981), p. 59.
10 This notion of wearing a 'bruised, underwater look' comes from Marie

Darrieussecq's novel *My Phantom Husband*, trans. Helen Stevenson (London, 1999), p. 35.

11 Daniel Wojcik, '"Polaroids from Heaven": Photography, Folk Religion, and the Miraculous Image Tradition at a Marian Apparition Site', *Journal of American Folklore* CIX/432 (1996), p. 135. I first became aware of the Polaroid's link to contemporary apparitions through a lecture by Beth Saunders, given at the Twenty-second Annual Conference of the Centre of Comparative Literature at the University of Toronto, 2011, entitled 'Photographic Faith: Marian Apparition Photographs and the Role of Photography in Popular Religious Belief'.

12 Wojcik, '"Polaroids from Heaven"', p. 130.

13 Ibid., p. 132.

14 Martin Barnes, *Shadow Catchers, Camera-less Photography* (London, 2010), p. 13.

15 Wojcik, '"Polaroids from Heaven"', p. 133.

16 Ibid.

17 Jean Baudrillard, 'The Precision of Simulacra', in *Art after Modernism: Rethinking Representation,* ed. Brian Wallis (New York, 1984), p. 37. As quoted in Wojcik, "Polaroids from Heaven", p. 140.

18 Wojcik, '"Polaroids from Heaven"', p. 135.

19 Andrew Ladis, *Giotto's O: Narrative, Figuration, and Pictorial Ingenuity in the Arena Chapel* (University Park, PA, 2008), p. 112.

20 Baudrillard, 'The Precision of Simulacra', p. 37.

21 Michel Alpatoff, 'The Parallelism of Giotto's Paduan Frescoes', in *Giotto: The Arena Chapel Frescoes,* ed. James Stubblebine (New York and London, 1969), pp. 156–169.

22 Alpatoff, 'The Parallelism of Giotto's Paduan Frescoes', pp. 162–3.

23 Kristeva, 'Giotto's Joy', p. 213.

24 Emily Dickinson, 'I heard a Fly buzz – when I died –', *The Complete Poems of Emily Dickinson*, ed. Thomas H. Johnson (New York, 1961), pp. 223–4.

25 Peter Wollen, 'Blue', *New Left Review* 6 (November / December, 2000), p. 125.

26 Vona Groarke, excerpt from 'Six Months', from her published collection *Spindrift* (Loughcrew, Oldcastle, Ireland, 2009), p. 40.

27 Proust scholars debate whether to call the 'Narrator' of *In Search of Lost Time* by the author's first name. The problem, since the book is neither fiction nor non-fiction, neither autobiography nor biography, neither novel nor philosophy, is impossible to solve. For this book, 'Marcel' seems to serve my purposes best.

28 Proust, *In Search of Lost Time,* V, *The Captive* and *The Fugitive* (New York, 1993), p. 1.

29 Michel Pastoureau, *Blue: The History of a Color,* trans. Markus I. Cruse (Princeton, NJ, and Oxford, 2001), p. 50.

30 Pastoureau, *Blue*, p. 51.

31 Marina Warner, *Alone of All Her Sex: The Myth and the Cult of the Virgin Mary* (London, 1976), p. 266.

32 Samira Makhmalbaf made *At Five in the Afternoon* when she was twenty-three years old. She first came to fame with her film *Apple*, made in 1997, when she was seventeen years old.

33 I am borrowing from the words of Robert Michael Pyle, who describes seeing a butterfly from the widespread group known as 'Blues', which was the focus of Navokov's highly-focused lepidoptery, as follows: 'I found Nabokov's Blue, a shred of the sky's thin air'. *Nabokov's Butterflies*, new translation from the Russian by Dmitri Nabokov, ed. and annotated by Brian Boyd and Robert Michael Pyle (Boston, 2000), p. 76.

34 Thank you to my student Ferdie Simon, who, in my seminar on 'Blue Mythologies', pointed out to me that the painting came from the 'Blue City'. Why the Jodhpur houses are painted blue has been subject to various 'mythologies', including the concept that it is the colour of the Brahmin caste or that the blue wash protects against insects or that the lovely light blue visually cools the city. Perhaps the answer is a braid of all three 'myths'.

35 Debra Diamond, Catherine Glynn and Karni Singh Jasol, with contributions by Jason Freitag and Rahul Jain, *Gardens and Cosmos: The Royal Paintings of Jodhpur* (London, 2008), p. 139.

36 Michael Taussig, 'Redeeming Indigo', *Theory, Culture & Society*, xxv/3 (2008), p. 3.

37 Ibid.

38 Taussig, 'Redeeming Indigo', p. 7.

39 Graham Martin, 'Through a penguin's eye', *New Scientist*, 14 March 1985, p. 31.

40 Kurt Johnson and Steve Coates, *Nabokov's Blues: The Scientific Odyssey of Literary Genius* (Cambridge, MA, 1999), p. 10.

41 Nabokov, 'From Nabokov's Cornell lectures, March, 1951', in *Nabokov's Butterflies,* p. 473.

42 Ibid.

43 Ibid.

44 Ibid.

45 Johnson and Coates, *Nabokov's Blues*, p. 35.

46 Ibid., p. 45.

47 Ibid.

48 Nabokov, as quoted in Johnson and Coates, *Nabokov's Blues*, p. 45.

49 Johnson and Coates, *Nabokov's Blues*, p. 13.

50 Vladimir Nabokov, *Pnin* (London, 2010), p. 111.

51 Martin Barnes, *Shadow Catchers* p. 11.

52 In regard to the pronunciation of the name Pnin, Nabokov explains: 'The "p" *is* sounded, that's all. But since the "pn" is mute in English

words starting with "pn", one is prone to insert a supporting "uh" sound –"Puh-nin" – which is wrong. To get the "pn" right, try the combination "Up North", or still better "Up Nina", leaving out the initial "u". Pnorth, Pnina, Pnin. Can you do that?' From a television interview with Robert Hughes in 1965, in Nabokov's *Strong Opinions* (London, 2011), p. 45.
53 Barnes, *Shadow Catchers*, p. 152.
54 Ibid.
55 Ibid.
56 Simon Ings, *The Eye: A Natural History* (London, 2007), p. 29.

3 UNWRAPPING *BLUE BOY*

1 As Ann Lawson Lucas notes: 'In *Pinocchio,* Collodi's use of "turchino" [as the adjective for describing the "Blue Fairy"] . . . requires special treatment . . . "Turchino" is an unusual word (unlike "blue"), meaning a deep or dark shade, while "turchinetto" is the noun for indigo or laundress's blue . . . These words are related to "Turchia" (Turkey), just as indigo is related to India. Thus, "indigo" both describes the colour and captures the special mood accurately [around issues of Otherness and the working class]. Needless to say, "turchino" has a cognate expression "farne dell turchine" which means "to be up to all sorts of tricks".'
   See Carlo Collodi, *The Adventures of Pinocchio*, Oxford World's Classics, trans., ed. and intro. Ann Lawson Lucas (London, 1996), p. 178, n. 46.
2 John Gage, *Colour and Meaning: Art Science and Symbolism* (London, 1999), p. 186.
3 Goethe, as cited by Gage, *Colour and Meaning*, p. 187.
4 Roland Barthes, *Empire of Signs*, trans. Richard Howard (New York, 1982), p. 45.
5 Ibid.
6 Rebecca Solnit, *A Field Guide to Getting Lost* (New York, 2005), p. 30.

4 ONE CAT, FOUR GIRLS, THREE BLUE-AND-WHITE POTS: WALPOLE'S 'SELIMA' AND SARGENT'S *DAUGHTERS OF EDWARD DARLEY BOIT*

1 Barbara Dayer Gallati, 'From Souvenir to High Art: Childhood on Display' in her *Great Expectations: John Singer Sargent Painting Children,* with contributions by Erica E. Hirshler and Richard Ormond (Brooklyn, 2005), p. 81.
2 Joséphin Péladan, 'L'ésthétique au Salon de 1883', *L'Artiste*, LIII (May, 1883) / 587, as cited by Barbara Dayer Gallati, p. 81. For more on Sargent and flowers, see Alison Syme, *A Touch of Blossom: John Singer Sargent and the Queer Flora of Fin-de-Siècle Art* (University Park, PA, 2010).

3 Gallati, 'From Souvenir to High Art', p. 81.
4 Ibid.
5 Susan Sidlauskas, *Body, Place, and Self in Nineteenth-Century Painting* (Cambridge, 2000), p. 61.
6 Ibid., p. 87.
7 Erica E. Hirshler, *Sargent's Daughters: A Biography of a Painting* (Boston, 2009), p. 77.
8 Ibid.
9 Sidlauskas, *Body, Place, and Self,* p. 87.
10 Hirshler, *Sargent's Daughters,* p. 82.
11 Amanda Vickery, reviewing 'Horace Walpole's Strawberry Hill', an exhibition at the Victoria and Albert Museum, London, 6 March – 4 July 2010, in *The Guardian,* 20 February 2010.
12 Ibid.
13 Ibid.
14 Christopher Frayling, *Horace Walpole's Cat* (London, 2009), p. 10.
15 As cited in the *Oxford English Dictionary* under 'gloomth'.
16 Ibid.
17 Of note is the fact that Walpole also coined the word 'serendipity' in 1754. He formed the word, according to the *Oxford English Dictionary,* 'upon the title of the fairy-tale "The Three Princes of Serendip", the heroes of which "were always making discoveries, by accidents and sagacity, of things they were not in quest of"'.
18 Frayling, *Walpole's Cat,* p. 12.
19 Ibid., p. 21.
20 Ibid., p. 19.
21 Ibid., p. 24.
22 Thomas Gray, 'On the Death of a Favourite Cat, Drowned in a Tub of Gold Fishes', as quoted by Frayling, *Horace Walpole's Cat,* p. 26.
23 Frayling, *Walpole's Cat,* p. 41. Although the cat is said to have drowned at Walpole's earlier home at 5 Arlington Street, London.
24 Ibid.

5 'A THING OF BLUE BEAUTY IS A GUILT FOR EVER'

1 Irène Némirovsky, *Suite Française,* translated by Sandra Smith (New York, 2006), p. 216.
2 Ibid., p. 33.
3 Sandra Smith, translator's note for Irène Némirovsky, *Suite Française,* p. ix.

6 MILK AND SUGAR ARE BLUE

1   Toni Morrison *The Bluest Eye* (New York, 1993), p. 23.
2   Roland Barthes, 'Wine and Milk', *Mythologies,* trans. Annette Lavers (London, 2000), p. 60.
3   Ibid.
4   See chapter Two, 'Blue is Joyful-Sad', for a short discussion of the indigo milk mushroom.
5   Roland Barthes, *The Neutral: Lecture Course at the Collège de France,* trans. Rosalind E. Krauss and Dennis Hollier (New York, 2005), p. 153.
6   Natasha Trethewey, from her poem 'Photography' in *Bellocq's Ophelia* (Saint Paul, MN, 2002), p. 43.
7   Morrison, *The Bluest Eye*, p. 50.
8   Roland Barthes, *Camera Lucida: Reflections on Photography,* trans. Richard Howard (New York, 1981), p. 91.
9   Irène Némirovsky, *Suite Française,* trans. Sandra Smith (New York, 2006), p. 33. See chapter 5, 'A thing of beauty is a guilt for ever'.

7 TIMBER, TIMBRE: *HEARING BLUE AGAIN*

1   Roland Barthes, 'Toys', *Mythologies,* trans. Annette Lavers (London, 2000), p. 54.
2   Chris Ofili, *The Blue Rider* (Berlin, 2005).
3   Louis Antwi, in Ofili, *The Blue Rider,* pp. 40–41.
4   Greg Tate, in Ofili, *The Blue Rider,* pp. 68–71.
5   Antwi, in Ofili, *The Blue Rider,* pp. 40–41.
6   Hannah Weitemeier, *Yves Klein: 1928-1962* (Cologne, 2001), p. 17.
7   Jean-Luc Nancy, *Listening,* trans. Charlotte Mandell (New York, 2007), p. 31.
8   As Leon S. Roudiez writes of Julia Kristeva's use of *jouissance*: in her 'vocabulary, sensual, sexual pleasure is covered by *plaisir;* "jouissance" is total joy or ecstasy . . . also, through the working of the signifier, this implies the presence of meaning (*jouissance = j'ouïs sens* = I heard meaning), requiring it by going beyond it.' Roudiez, 'Introduction' to Julia Kristeva's *Desire in Language: A Semiotic Approach to Literature and Art*, edited by Leon S. Roudiez, trans. Thomas Gora, Alice Jardine and Leon S. Roudiez (Columbia, NY, 1980), p. 16. I want to thank David Richardson, who, after a lecture I gave on the *timbre* of trees, got me thinking about the word in French as also meaning 'stamp'.
9   Jimi Hendrix, 'Purple Haze', 1966–7.

8 A BOLT FROM THE BLUE

1 One of my former students, the artist Wendy Chen, in a seminar paper on the beds of the late Cuban–American artist Félix Gonzáles-Torres noted that 'the bed is a hatchery for dreams'.

2 Michael Balint, 'Flying Dreams and the Dream Screen' in *Thrills and Regressions* (New York, 1959), p. 75.

3 Sigmund Freud, *Civilization and Its Discontents* in *The Standard Edition of the Complete Psychological Works of Sigmund Freud*, vol. xxi (London, 2001), p. 64. The emphasis on 'eternity' is mine.

4 Freud came up with the term in his correspondence with Romain Rolland. See Ranjana Khanna, *Dark Continents: Psychoanalysis and Colonialism* (Durham and London, 2003), pp. 91–95.

5 Gauguin, *Cahier pour Aline*, as quoted in Herschel B. Chipp, *Theories of Modern Art* (Berkeley, CA, 1992), p. 69.

6 Daniel Wildenstein, *Gauguin: A Savage in the Making, Catalogue Raisonné (1873–1888)*, vol. I (Milan, 2002), p. 87.

7 Wildenstein, *Gauguin*, p. 86.

8 Gauguin, as quoted in Belinda Thomson, *Gauguin by Himself* (Edison, NJ, 2001), p. 255.

9 Linda Nochlin, *Politics of Vision: Essays on Nineteenth-century Art and Society* (Boulder, CO, and Oxford, 1991), p. 91. See also John Hutton, 'The Clown at the Ball: Manet's Masked Ball at the Opera', *The Oxford Art Journal*, X/2 (1987), pp. 76–94.

10 Wildenstein, *Gauguin*, p. 89.

11 In regard to the genesis of his famous painting *Where Do We Come From? What Are We? Where Are We Going* (1897–8), Gauguin 'wrote to the critic André Fontainas that it flowed out, at night and in "total silence," as "my eyes close, to *see without comprehending* the dream in the infinite space before me."' See Deborah Silverman, *Van Gogh and Gauguin: The Search for Sacred Art* (New York, 2000), p. 389.

12 Nancy Mowll Matthews, *Paul Gauguin: An Erotic Life* (New Haven, CT, and London, 2001), p. 127.

13 Gauguin, *Cahier pours Aline,* as quoted in Chipp, *Theories of Modern Art*, p. 69.

14 Ibid.

15 Ibid.

16 Charles Stuckey, as quoted in Wildenstein, *Gauguin*, p. 87.

17 Wildenstein, *Gauguin*, p. 422.

18 W. Somerset Maugham, *The Moon and Sixpence* (New York, 1944), p. 191.

19 Lynne Huffer, *Maternal Pasts, Feminist Futures: Nostalgia, Ethics and the Question of Difference* (Stanford, CA, 1998), p. 14.

20 Maugham, *The Moon and Sixpence*, pp. 150–51.

21 Rebecca Solnit, *A Field Guide to Getting Lost* (New York, 2005), p. 29.
22 Roland Barthes, *Camera Lucida: Reflections on Photography* (New York, 1981), p. 71. Barthes is writing about his own mother, towards the end of her life she had become his 'child'.
23 In *Camera Lucida,* Barthes writes of looking at photographs through 'the brightness' of his mother's eyes . . . the blue-green of her pupils [*prunelles*]' (p. 66). It is unclear whether Barthes meant irises here or not. The pupil is not coloured. Nevertheless, as a hole in the centre of the iris, which allows light to enter, the pupil is in keeping with the 'loss' that Barthes is after.
24 David Lowenthal, *The Past is a Foreign Country* (Cambridge, 1985).
25 Barthes, *Camera Lucida*, p. 26.
26 Natasha Trethewey, from her poem 'December 1911' in *Bellocq's Ophelia* (Saint Paul, MN, 2002), p. 30.
27 Barthes, *Camera Lucida*, p. 81.

9 SEMIOCLASM CYANOCLASM

 1 As a student of White, I received the 'gift' of Barthes in my first semi-nar led by White and James Clifford, under the title of 'Theory and Methods', in the well- known program known as the 'History of Consciousness'.
 2 Roland Barthes, *Mythologies*, trans. Annette Lavers (London, 2000), p. 9.
 3 Barthes' attachment to rhetoric is taken up more fully in chapter Twelve, 'To Blue'.
 4 Barthes, *Mythologies*, pp. 55–56.
 5 Barthes, Ibid., p, 53.
 6 Translator's note, in *Mythologies,* bottom of p. 74.
 7 Ibid., p. 75
 8 Ibid., p. 77.
 9 Ibid., p. 75.
10 Ibid., p. 76.
11 Ibid., p. 62.
12 Ibid., p. 63.
13 Ibid., p. 89.
14 Ibid., p. 89.
15 In French, the word for goddess is *déesse*.
16 Barthes, *Mythologies*, p. 90.

10 LIKE A STOCKING: *TWO PATHS OF METAPHOR AND METONYMY*

1 This chapter's understanding of metaphor and metonymy has been
   enhanced by a conversation with the theorist and poet David Marriott,
   who was responding to a lecture that I gave on the colour blue at the
   San Francisco Art Institute in 2011.

2 As mentioned in chapter Two, 'Blue is Joyful-Sad', it is a matter of debate
   to refer to the 'Narrator' of *In Search of Lost Time* as 'Marcel'. 'Marcel'
   seems especially appropriate for the approach of *Blue Mythologies*, but
   even more so for this chapter's treatment of *The Captive* (volume v of
   the *Search*). For it is in *The Captive* that the name 'Marcel' leaks out
   through the lips of Albertine when addressing the 'Narrator'. Indeed, it
   does seem to come to the reader, after many pages and volumes of the
   Search, 'out of the blue'. Whether or not this 'slip' was intentional is
   unknown because the volume was published posthumously.

3 Marcel Proust, *In Search of Lost Time,* trans. C. K. Scott-Moncrieff and
   Terence Kilmartin, revised by D. J. Enright, v, *The Captive* and *The
   Fugitive* (New York, 1993), p. 14.

4 Hayden White, 'Hayden White in Conversation with Carol Mavor',
   *immediations: The Courtauld Institute of Art Journal of Postgraduate
   Research,* ii/2 (2009), p. 105.

5 Ibid.

6 Kieślowski film and the blue lolly is taken up in chapter Seventeen,
   'A Blue Lollipop'.

7 White, 'Hayden White in Conversation with Carol Mavor', p. 105.

8 Julia Kristeva, *Time and Sense: The Experience of Literature,* trans. Ross
   Guberman (New York, 1996), p. 212.

9 Natasha Trethewey, from her poem 'Bellocq's Ophelia' in *Bellocq's
   Ophelia* (Saint Paul, MN, 2002), p. 3.

10 Roland Barthes, 'Longtemps, je me suis couché de bonne heure . . .',
   in *The Rustle of Language,* trans. Richard Howard (Berkeley and Los
   Angeles, CA, 1989), p. 278.

11 Ibid.

12 Marcel Proust, *In Search of Lost Time,* trans. C. K. Scott-Moncrieff and
   Terence Kilmartin, revised by D. J. Enright, i, *Swann's Way* (New York,
   1993), p. 64.

13 Roland Barthes, 'Dare to Be Lazy', in *The Grain of the Voice: Interviews
   1962–1980,* trans. Linda Coverdale (New York, 1985), p. 343.

14 Ibid.

15 Tim Robison, *Oileán Árann: A Companion to the Map of the Aran
   Islands* (Galway, Ireland, 1996), p. 84.

16 From the British Library's notes accompanying an original (nearly
   complete) copy of Atkins's *British Algae* (Special Collections).

17 This phrase is the title of a book on representations of the natural world in the mid-nineteenth century, with an emphasis on Atkins's cyanotypes and other related works between science and art. See Carol Armstrong and Catherine De Zegher, *Ocean Flowers: Impressions from Nature* (Princeton, NJ, 2004).

18 Barthes, 'Dare to Be Lazy', p. 343.

11 BLUE LESSONS: *A PATCH OF BLUE, A BLUE CARDIGAN BUTTONED AND A ROBIN'S EGG*

1 Sally Hobart Alexander, *Do you remember the color blue?* (New York, 2000), p. 67.

2 In Canada, a *bleuet* is a blueberry.

3 See the memoir by the synaesthete with Savant Syndrome by Daniel Tammet, *Born on a Blue Day* (London, 2006).

4 Richard E. Cytowic and David M. Eagleman, *Wednesday is Indigo Blue: Discovering the Brain of Synesthesia* (Cambridge, MA, 2009).

5 Patricia Lynne Duffy, *Blue Cats and Chartreuse Kittens: How Synethetes Color Their World* (New York, 2001).

6 Jamie Ward, *The Frog Who Croaked Blue: Synesthesia and the Mixing of the Senses* (London, 2009).

7 Laurie Colwin, ' Mr Parker', as collected in her *Passion and Affect* (New York, 1995), pp. 127–133.

8 Ibid., p. 129.

9 Ibid., p. 128.

10 Ibid., p. 129.

11 Emily Dickinson, 'The Brain – is wider than the Sky', the first line to her poem, *circa* 1866, in *The Complete Poems of Emily Dickinson,* ed. Thomas H. Johnson (Boston, 1961), p. 312.

12 Colwin, 'Mr Parker', p. 129.

13 Ibid., p. 130.

14 Ibid.

15 Ibid., p. 127.

16 Ibid.

17 Ibid., p. 128.

18 Ibid., p. 130.

19 Philina A. English and Robert Montgomerie, 'Robin's egg blue: does egg color influence male parental care?', *Behavioral Ecology and Sociobiology*, LXV (2011), p. 1029.

20 Ibid., pp. 1029–36.

12 TO BLUE: *HELEN CHADWICK'S OVAL COURT*

1   Marie Darrieussecq uses Björk's song as an epigraph to her fine novel, *Breathing Underwater*, trans. Linda Coverdale (London, 2002).

2   Roland Barthes, 'Death of the Author', in *Image-Music-Text,* trans. Stephen Heath (New York, 1977), p. 145. Although the publishing date for 'The Death of the Author' is usually cited as 1968, the more accurate date is 1967. As Geoffrey Batchen notes: 'Barthes's text was first published in English (having been translated by Richard Howard) in the United States, appearing in 1967 as part of *Aspen,* number 5 + 6, an art project posing as a magazine. This issue consisted of twenty-eight numbered items gathered in a box, including essays by Barthes, Susan Sontag and George Kubler'. See Geoffrey Batchen, ed., *Photography Degree Zero: Reflection on Roland Barthes's 'Camera Lucida'* (Cambridge, MA, and London, 2009), n. 22, p. 23.

3   According to the *Oxford English Dictionary*, the verb *to blue* can mean 'to make blue', as in to heat metal to make it blue. *To blue* linen is to starch it. An obsolete meaning of *to blue,* from the eighteenth century, is 'to blush'. *To blue* can also mean 'to blow through money' or 'to make a mess of'.

4   Roland Barthes, 'To Write: An Intransitive Verb?', *The Rustle of Language,* trans. Richard Howard (Berkeley and Los Angeles, CA, 1989), pp. 11–21.

5   Helen Chadwick, *Enfleshings*, with an essay by Marina Warner entitled 'In the Garden of Delights', as quoted by Warner (New York, 1989), p. 47.

6   Chadwick, *Enfleshings*, p. 62.

7   Warner, 'In the Garden of Delights', in Chadwick, *Enfleshings,* p. 39.

8   Ibid. p. 56.

9   Ibid.

10   Ibid., p. 48. As Warner writes, 'the notorious show of rump by Mlle O'Murphy in several Boucher paintings is reproduced by the swimming figure'.

11   Brian Massumi, 'Too-blue: Color-Patch for an Expanded Empiricism', in *Parable for the Virtual: Movement, Affect, Sensation* (Durham, NC, and London), p. 210.

12   Roland Barthes, *La Chambre claire: Note sur la photographie* (Paris, 1980), p. 49. Translation is mine. In English, *Camera Lucida: Reflections on Photography*, trans. Richard Howard (New York, 1981), p. 27. Howard translates this passage as 'sting, speck, cut, little hole,' p. 27.

13 'A FOGGY LULLABY'

1 Micheal Pastoureau, *Blue: The History of a Color,* trans. Markus I. Cruse (Princeton, NJ, and Oxford, 2001), p. 140.
2 Ibid.

14 WORDS FAIL

1 Roland Barthes, *Empire of Signs*, trans. Richard Howard (New York, 1982), p. 89.
2 Johann Wolfgang von Goethe, *The Sorrows of Young Werther,* trans. Michael Hulse (London, 1989), pp. 67–8.
3 Goethe, *The Sorrows of Young Werther*, p. 92.
4 Roland Barthes, *A Lover's Discourse: Fragments*, trans. Richard Howard (New York, 1978), p. 128.
5 Glynis Ridley, *Clara's Grand Tour: Travels with a Rhinoceros in Eighteenth-Century Europe* (New York, 2004), p. 180.
6 Anne Higonnet, *Berthe Morisot* (Berkeley, CA, 1995), p. 92.

15 A BLUE FAWN'S EYE

1 Rebecca Solnit, *A Field Guide to Getting Lost* (New York, 2005), p. 37.
2 Helen Sear, from a poem written to accompanying her photograph, when exhibited, *The Pond*, 2011.
3 Jean-Luc Nancy, *The Fall of Sleep*, trans. Charlotte Mandell (Fordham, NY, 2007), p. 30.
4 Solnit, *A Field Guide to Getting Lost*, p. 29.
5 Brian Massumi, 'Too-blue: Color-Patch for an Expanded Empiricism', in *Parable for the Virtual: Movement, Affect, Sensation* (Durham, NC, and London), p. 210.
6 John Banville, *The Sea* (London, 2005), p. 215.
7 Novalis, *Henry von Ofterdingen*, trans. Palmer Hitty (Prospect Heights, IL, 1990), p. 98. Part novel, part fairy tale, and part poem, this magical book was first published posthumously in 1802. See also chapter Three, 'Unwrapping *Blue Boy*'.
8 Banville, *The Sea*, p. 215.
9 During the Baroque period, we find the Virgin turning gold. See Michel Pastoureau, *Blue: The History of a Color,* trans. Markus I. Cruse (Princeton, NJ, and Oxford, 2001), p. 55.
10 Nicolas Abraham and Mária Török, 'Mourning *or* Melancholia: Introjection *versus* Incorporation' in Abraham and Török, *The Shell and the Kernel: Renewals of Psychoanalysis*, vol. I, trans. Nicholas T. Rand (Chicago, 1994), p. 130.
11 Ibid.

12 Karl Abraham (1877–1925), whose work closely follows Freud's own discussion of the oral stage. See Abraham's 'The Influence of Oral Eroticism on Character Formation' in *Selected Papers* (New York, (1924), pp. 393–406.

13 Daniel Birnbaum and Anders Olsson, quoting Karl Abraham, in *As a Weasel Sucks Eggs: An Essay on Melancholy and Cannibalism*, trans. Brian Manning Delaney (Berlin and New York, 2008), p. 59.

14 Birnbaum and Olsson, quoting Freud, in *As a Weasel Sucks Eggs*, p. 62.

15 Birnbaum and Olsson, quoting Karl Abraham, in *As a Weasel Sucks Eggs*, p. 60.

16 'BLUE ALBERTINE' AND 'BLUE ARIANE' (*MARCEL PROUST AND CHANTAL AKERMAN*)

1 Proust, *The Captive*, p. 120.

2 Proust, *Swann's Way*, p. 60.

3 Ibid., p. 63.

4 Julia Kristeva, *Time and Sense: Proust and the Experience of Literature*, trans. Ross Guberman (New York, 1998), p. 5.

5 Proust, *The Captive*, p. 14.

6 Ibid., p. 226.

7 Ibid., p. 81.

8 Ibid., p. 81.

9 Ibid., p. 14.

10 Rebecca Solnit, *A Field Guide to Getting Lost* (New York, 2005), p. 29.

11 Proust, *The Captive*, p. 520.

12 Longhi's painting is discussed in chapter Fourteen, 'Words Fail'.

13 From Anne Garreta's introduction to Jacqueline Rose's presentation on 13 April 2005, Duke University, Durham, North Carolina. Rose was reading from her novel *Albertine*.

14 Valerie Steele, *Paris Fashion: A Cultural History* (New York and Oxford, 1988), p. 215.

15 Guillermo de Osma, *Mariano Fortuny: His Life and Work* (New York, 1985), p. 110.

16 Proust, *The Captive*, p. 531.

17 Steele, *Paris Fashion: A Cultural History*, p. 215.

18 Wendy Ligon Smith, 'Guest Lecture', spring semester, 2012, for my course 'Art in the Time of Proust' at the University of Manchester.

19 Marcel Proust, *In Search of Lost Time*, trans. C. K. Scott-Moncrieff and Terence Kilmartin, revised by D. J. Enright, v, *The Captive* and *The Fugitive* (New York, 1993), p. 531.

20 Arthur Lucas and Joyce Plesters, 'Titian's *Bacchus and Ariadne*', *National Gallery Technical Bulletin*, volume II (London, 1978), p. 40.

21 Ibid.

22 Ibid.

23 Ibid.

24 Of note, is the fact that one cannot help but colour Albertine with Marcel's lover-chauffeur-secretary, Alfred Agostinelli. He fell from the sky and into the sea in a plane named *Le Cygne* – the same name given to Albertine's yacht in the novel.

25 Barthes, *A Lover's Discourse, Fragments*, trans. Richard Howard (New York, 1978), p. 88.

26 Proust, *The Captive*, p. 165.

27 Ibid., p. 87.

28 Ibid., pp. 87–8.

29 Colette, *For a Flower Album,* trans. Roger Semhouse (New York, 1959), p. 35.

30 Sharman Apt Russell, *Anatomy of a Rose* (New York, 2002), p. 162.

31 Proust, *The Captive*, p. 500.

32 Ibid.

33 John Gage, *Colour and Meaning: Art Science and Symbolism* (London, 1999), p. 13.

17 A BLUE LOLLIPOP (*KRZYSZTOF KIEŚLOWSKI*)

1 Marie Darrieussecq's novel *My Phantom Husband*, trans. Helen Stevenson (London, 1999), p. 35. See chapter Two, 'Blue is Joyful-Sad'.

2 Gabriel García Márquez, *Love in the Time of Cholera*, trans. Edith Grossman (New York, 1997), p. 114.

3 Julia Kristeva, 'Giotto's Joy', *Desire in Language: A Semiotic Approach to Literature and Art,* trans. Thomas Gora, Alice Jardine and Leon S. Roudiez (New York, 1980), p. 219.

4 Francesca Woodman, from her journal (from August 1975 to 31 December 1975), extracts edited by her father George Woodman, in *Francesca Woodman: Scattered in Space and Time* (London, 2006). Please note that the journal pages are at the end of the volume and are unpaginated.

5 Marcel Proust, *Marcel Proust on Art and Literature*, trans. Sylvia Townsend Warner (New York, 1997), p. 358.

6 See chapter Fifteen, 'A Blue Fawn's Eye'.

7 Nicolas Abraham and Mária Török, 'Mourning *or* Melancholia: Introjection *versus* Incorporation' in Abraham and Török, *The Shell and the Kernel: Renewals of Psychoanalysis*, vol. I, trans. Nicholas T. Rand (Chicago, 1994), pp. 127–8.

8 Daniel Birnbaum and Anders Olsson, *As a Weasel Sucks Eggs: An Essay on Melancholy and Cannibalism,* trans. Brian Manning Delaney (Berlin and New York), p. 59.

9 Daniel Birnbaum and Anders Olsson, quoting Karl Abraham, in *As a*

Weasel Sucks Eggs: An Essay on Melancholy and Cannibalism (Berlin and New York, 2008), p. 60.

10 Proust, *The Captive*, p. 22.

18 'O BLUE'

1 Vladimir Nabokov, *Speak, Memory: An Autobiography Revisited* (London, 1998), p. 17.

2 Rebecca Solnit, *A Field Guide to Getting Lost* (New York, 2005). p. 29.

3 Julia Kristeva, 'Giotto's Joy', *Desire in Language: A Semiotic Approach to Literature and Art,* translated by Thomas Gora, Alice Jardine and Leon S. Roudiez (New York, 1980), p. 221.

4 Mark Godfrey, from Tate Modern's leaflet text accompanying the exhibition *Francis Alÿs, A Story of Deception*, 15 June–5 September 2010 (London, 2010), p. 4.

5 Tim Robinson, from his lecture, 'A Land Without Shortcuts', as the Parnell Visiting Fellow for 2011, at Magdalene College, University of Cambridge.

6 Nan Rosenthal, 'Assisted Levitation: The Art of Yves Klein', in *Yves Klein, 1928–1962, A Retrospective*, catalogue from the exhibition at the Rice Museum, Houston, Texas, 5 February – 2 May 1982 (New York, 1982), p. 123.

19 VENICE IS A WET MAP: *TADZIO IN BLUE*

1 Guillermo de Osman, *Mariano Fortuny: His Life and Work* (New York, 1985), p. 99.

2 Delphine Desveaux, *Fortuny*, trans. Harriet Mason (London,1998), p. 13.

3 Wendy Ligon Smith, Wendy Ligon Smith 'Guest Lecture', spring semester 2012, for the author's course 'Art in the Time of Proust', at the University of Manchester.

4 'Folding Landscapes' is a publishing house and information centre with a strong eye on the Aran Islands, run by Máiréad Robinson and the writer Tim Robinson. See chapter Twenty-one, 'Aran is a Blue Place Where it is Hard to Find Anything Missing'.

5 Peter Ackroyd, *Venice: Pure City* (London, 2010), p. 23.

6 Robert Coover, *Pinocchio in Venice* (London, 1991), p. 26.

7 Ibid., p. 27.

8 From the Nicolas Roeg film *Don't Look Now* (2003), based on the story by Daphne du Maurier.

9 Thomas Mann, *Death in Venice, in Death in Venice and Other Stories*, translated by David Luke (London, 1998), p. 213.

10 Mann, *Death in Venice,* p. 202.

11 Ibid., p. 259.

12 Ibid., p. 219.
13 Gilbert Adair, *The Real Tadzio: Thomas Mann's 'Death in Venice' and the Boy Who Inspired It* (London, 2003), p. 12.
14 Adair, *The Real Tadzio*, p. 17.
15 Mann, *Death in Venice*, p. 220.
16 James Crump, *F. Holland Day: Suffering the Ideal* (Santa Fe, NM, 1995), p. 26.
17 Crump, ibid., p. 10.
18 I thank Alison Criddle for helping me to think through Caravaggio's *Narcissus* as a boyish image of light writing.
19 Roland Barthes, *The Pleasure of the Text*, trans. Richard Miller (New York, 1975), p. 4.
20 Julia Kristeva, *Powers of Horror: An Essay on Abjection,* trans. Leon S. Roudiez (New York, 1982), p. 4.
21 Charles Wehrenberg, *Mississippi Blue: Henry P. Bosse and his Views on the Mississippi River, Between Minneapolis and St. Louis, 1883–1891* (Santa Fe, NM, 2002), pp. 11–12.
22 Ibid., p. 13.
23 Rebecca Solnit, *A Field Guide to Getting Lost* (New York, 2005), p. 35.
24 Wehrenberg, *Mississippi Blue*, p. 7.
25 Marcel Proust, *In Search of Lost Time,* trans. C. K. Scott-Moncrieff and Terence Kilmartin, revised by D. J. Enright, I, *Swann's Way* (New York, 1993), p. 64. For a lengthier discussion of this passage, see chapter Ten, 'Like a Stocking'.
26 Peter Ackroyd, *Venice*, p. 35.
27 Ibid.
28 Mann, *Death in Venice*.
29 Ibid., p. 263.
30 Ibid., p. 266.
31 Kristeva, *Powers of Horror*, p. 3.
32 Mann, *Death in Venice*, p. 212.

20 DOMESTIC BLUES: AGNÈS VARDA'S *LE BONHEUR*

1 Colm Tóibín, 'In Lovely Blueness: Adventures in Troubled Light', citing Johann Wolfgang von Goethe's 1810 *Theory of Colours*. In 2004 Tóibín curated an exhibition at the Chester Beatty Library in Dublin called *Blue* which consisted of blue objects from the collection. Tóibín's essay is the introduction to the catalogue and can be found on Tóibín's website.
2 From the DVD, 'special feature', *Le Bonheur: The People of Fontenay Respond*, part of *The Agnès Varda Collection*, volume I, with *La Pointe Courte, Cléo from 5 to 7, Le Bonheur* and *The Gleaners and I* (France, Artificial Eye, 2000).

3 François is played by the French television star Jean-Claude Drouot. Thérèse is played by Claire Drouot, and their children, Sandrine and Olivier, play their filmic offspring.

4 See chapter Seven, 'Timbre, Timber'.

5 Mary Kelly, in an interview with Hal Foster, entitled 'That Obscure Subject of Desire', in *Interim* (New York, 1990), p. 55; reprinted in Mary Kelly, *Imaging Desire* (Cambridge, MA, 1996), p. 170.

6 See Amy Taubin, *'Le Bonheur:* Splendor in the Grass', an online review that is on the website for Criterion films (posted 21 January 2008).

7 Stephen Bann, *Paul Delaroche: History Painted* (London, 1997), p. 263.

8 Ibid.

9 David Lomas, 'Philosophy in Painting: André Masson's *Ophelia* (1937)', in *The Colour of My Dreams: The Surrealist Revolution in Art* (Vancouver, 2011), p. 83.

10 Charlotte Perkins Gilman, 'The Yellow Wall-Paper' in *The Yellow Wall-Paper and Other Stories* (Oxford, 2009), p. 14.

11 This is how Van Gogh's sunflowers were described to me by Kevin Parker.

12 Sara Ahmed, *The Promise of Happiness* (Durham, NC, and London, 2010), p. 46.

13 William Gass, *On Being Blue: A Philosophical Inquiry* (Boston, 1976), p. 3.

14 Derek Jarman, *Chroma* (London, 200), p. 115.

15 Julia Kristeva, 'Giotto's Joy' in *Desire in Language: A Semiotic Approach to Literature and Art,* edited by Leon S. Roudiez, translated by Thomas Gora, Alice Jardine and Leon S. Roudiez (New York, 1980), p. 213.

21 ARAN IS A BLUE PLACE WHERE IT IS HARD TO FIND ANYTHING MISSING

1 Tim Robinson, *Stones of Aran: Pilgrimage* (London: 2008), p. 8.

2 From the famed documentary by Robert J. Flaherty, *Man of Aran,* 1934.

3 Truer to Irish heritage, it would be more appropriate to call the big island of Inis Mór by its proper name of 'Árainn'. For details on the correct names of the Aran Islands, see Tim Robinson, *Stones of Aran,* p. 8.

4 Sean Scully, *Sean Scully: Walls of Aran, Introduction* by Colm Tóibín, and *Afterword* by Sean Scully (London, 2007), p. 122.

5 Tim Robinson, *Stones of Aran,* p. 235.

6 Patricia Patterson, 'Aran Kitchens, Aran Sweaters', *Heresies (issue 4): Women's Traditional Arts / The Politics of Aesthetics,* 1/4 (1978), p. 89.

7 Patterson, 'Aran Kitchens, Aran Sweaters', p. 92.

8 J. M. Synge, 'The Aran Islands', in *The Complete Works of J. M. Synge* (London, 2008), p. 331.

9 William Gass, *On Being Blue: A Philosophical Inquiry* (Boston, 1976), p. 76.

10 Máiréad Robinson is the partner of the writer Tim Robinson. Together, they are the founders of 'Folding Landscapes', a specialist publishing house and information resource centre dealing with three areas of particular interest and beauty around Galway Bay: the Aran Islands, the Burren and Connemara.

11 Patterson and Farber, 'Kitchen Without Kitsch', p. 48.

12 Ibid., p. 49.

13 Chantal Akerman, 'Chantal Akerman on *Jeanne Dielman*: Excerpts from an Interview with *Camera Obscura*, November 1976', *Camera Obscura,* II (Fall 1977), p. 119.

14 Ibid.

15 Grant Holcomb, Introduction to the catalogue for Patricia Patterson's exhibition *The Rabbit and the Kiss*, 24 September–13 November 1983, San Diego Museum of Art, California (1983), p. 6.

16 Colm Tóibín, *Sean Scully: Walls of Aran,* p. 11.

17 Roland Barthes, *The Pleasure of the Text,* trans. Richard Miller (New York, 1975), pp. 66–67.

18 Colm Tóibín, *Sean Scully: Walls of Aran*, p. 82.

22 IN LIEU OF A BLUE ENDING: *UN-KNITTING A CERULEAN JUMPER*

1 Tim Robinson, *Stones of Aran: Pilgrimage* (London, 2008), p. 16.

2 Louis Marin, *Utopics: The Semiological Play of Textual Space*, trans. Robert A. Vollrath (Atlantic Highlands, NJ, 1990), p. xv.

3 I am especially influenced by Marin's *Utopics.*

4 Thomas More, *Utopia*, ed. George M. Logan and Robert Adams (Cambridge, 1975), p. xi.

5 Fredric Jameson, 'The Politics of Utopia', *New Left Review*, XXV (January–February 2004), p. 41.

6 Roland Barthes, 'Dare to Be Lazy', in *The Grain of the Voice: Interviews, 1962–1980*, trans. Linda Coverdale (Berkeley and Los Angeles, CA, 1991), pp. 340–41.

7 Francis Alÿs, from an interview with Russell Ferguson, in *Francis Alÿs* (London, 2008), p. 29.

ACKNOWLEDGEMENTS

BLUE MYTHOLOGIES began as a seminar full of luminous students who inspired me. Together, we went on a blue pilgrimage. In my memory, the 'street was entirely paved with sapphire blue water, cooled by warm breezes and of a colour so durable that my tired eyes might rest their gaze upon it in search of relaxation without fear of its blanching' (Marcel Proust). I thank all of those students who came along for the journey.

I am especially grateful to Ali Criddle and Sophie Preston, who have listened to most of these pages and have made it a better book.

I have lectured from this book far and wide and my audiences have kept me on my toes at the following institutions: San Francisco Art Institute, Duke University, University of Toronto, University of Cambridge, Royal College of Art, The Photographers' Gallery (London), University of York, University of Essex, University of Birmingham, London College of Communication and the Courtauld Institute of Art.

A turning point for this book came while lecturing on the colour blue as the 2011 Northrop Frye Professor at the University of Toronto. I benefited greatly from my audience there. In particular, I will forever be indebted to my glorious conversations (with a taste for science) with Peter N. Burns and some real heart-to-hearts with Eva-Lynn Jagoe (with a taste for the novel).

An interview on the CBC (Canadian Broadcasting Company) for their *Sunday Edition* programme on 1 May 2011 opened up my ears to blue in the earlier stages of *Blue Mythologies*.

Special keys to unlocking various blues have been generously given to me by Kevin Parker, Esther Teichmann, Wendy Ligon Smith, Alison Connolly (*les clés du français*), Vona Groarke, Tim and Máiréad Robinson and Amy Ruth Buchanan.

My father sent us to Venice so that Kevin and I could experience the liquid blue streets in our own gondola.

The concept of a book on blue belongs to Michael Leaman. (It was a good idea, like so many of Michael's projects at Reaktion Books.) He has also been a very patient supporter of the project.

I am very grateful for a British Academy Small Research Grant that helped to support the acquisition of enough blue images.

And last but not least, thanks goes to my three boys (Ollie, Augie and Ambie), who, like it or not, were born into a gender that is often coloured blue.

And to Kevin once more, because once is never enough. He makes it all passionately possible, whether he is standing with me before a blue-veiled Bellini *Madonna* in Venice, tolerating my tears at the joy that I feel in Padua as I am struck by Giotto's blue, cracking the azure copper-sulphate crystals beneath our feet as we walk through Roger Hiorns's strange London 'grotto', or serving me blueberries under the grey skies of Manchester.

PHOTO ACKNOWLEDGEMENTS

The author and the publishers wish to express their thanks to the below sources of illustrative material and /or permission to reproduce it.

Collection of the author: p. 117; from the author's notebook 2011: pp. 130–31; Barber Institute of Fine Arts, Birmingham: pp. 13; The Bridgeman Art Library: p. 16 (Chapel of the Cemetery, Monterchi, Italy), 113 (Private Collection, Paris, France/Giraudon); © Trustees of the British Museum, London: p. 106; courtesy of the Helen Chadwick Estate: pp. 98, 101; photo: Duke of Derby Collection, Knowsley Estate: p. 53; permission courtesy of Annabel Dover: pp. 80, 83; permission courtesy of Bernard Faucon: p. 37; permission courtesy of Adam Fuss and the Frankel Gallery: p. 41; © Roger Hiorns, installation commissioned and produced by ArtAngel: pp. 42–3 (photo: author's own); The Huntingdon Library, California: p. 44; Library of Congress, Washington, DC: pp. 149–50, 153; Louvre, Paris/RMN/Hervé Lewandowski: p. 160; © Succession H. Matisse/DACS 2013: p. 58 (photo: Archives H. Matisse); Carol Mavor: p. 6; The Menil Collection, Houston/© ADAGP, Paris and DACS, London 2013: p. 18 (photo: Hickey-Robertston, Houston); Mehrangarh Museum Trust, Jodphur, Rajasthan, India and His Highness Maharaja Gaj Singh of Jodhpur: p. 32; The Metropolitan Museum of Art/© Sucession Miro/ADAGP, Paris and DACS, London 2013: p. 66; Museo de Bellas Artes, Sevilla: p. 31; Museo de San Joaquin y Santa Ana, Valladolid, Spain: p. 119 (photo: Imagen M.A.S); photograph © 2013 Museum of Fine Arts, Boston: p. 48; Fonds Irène Némirovsky/IMEC Images: p. 55; New York Public Library: pp. 87–9; © The National Gallery, London: pp. 108–9, 125; © Chris Ofili/Contemporary Fine Arts, Berlin: p. 63 (Jochen Littkemann Berlin); Ordrupgaard, Copenhagen: p. 69 (Pernille Klemp); permission courtesy of Patricia Patterson: pp. 167, 173; Collection Centre Pompidou, photo: RMN/Adam Rzepka/©ADAGP, Paris and DACS, London 2013: p. 84; Rijksmuseum, Netherlands: p. 169; permission courtesy of Alan Rockefeller: p. 33; permission courtesy of Helen Sear: p. 114; permission courtesy of Esther Teichmann: p. 25; Victoria and Albert Museum, London: pp. 102, 104, 146; permission courtesy of Betty and George Woodman: p. 135; USACE Technical Library/U.S. Corps of Engineers, Rock Island District: p. 154.

INDEX

Page numbers in *italics* indicate illustrations.